# The Civil Rights Act of 1964

LANDMARK LEGISLATION

# The Civil Rights Act of 1964

Susan Dudley Gold

**Marshall Cavendish**
Benchmark
New York

*Dedicated to my father, Edward E. Dudley, who taught me the importance of fairness and justice.*

*With special thanks to Catherine McGlone, Esq., for reviewing the text of this book.*

This publication represents the opinions and views of the author based on her personal experience, knowledge, and research. The information in this book serves as a general guide only. The author and publisher have used their best efforts in preparing this book and disclaim liability rising directly and indirectly from the use and application of this book.

Other Marshall Cavendish Offices:
Marshall Cavendish International (Asia) Private Limited, 1 New Industrial Road, Singapore 536196 • Marshall Cavendish International (Thailand) Co. Ltd. 253 Asoke, 12th Flr, Sukhumvit 21 Road, Klongtoey Nua, Wattana, Bangkok 10110, Thailand • Marshall Cavendish (Malaysia) Sdn Bhd, Times Subang, Lot 46, Subang Hi-Tech Industrial Park, Batu Tiga, 40000 Shah Alam, Selangor Darul Ehsan, Malaysia
Marshall Cavendish is a trademark of Times Publishing Limited

All websites were available and accurate when this book was sent to press.

Library of Congress Cataloging-in-Publication Data
Gold, Susan Dudley.
The Civil Rights Act of 1964 / by Susan Dudley Gold.
p. cm. — (Landmark legislation)
Includes bibliographical references and index.
ISBN 978-1-60870-040-0
1. United States. Civil Rights Act of 1964—Juvenile literature.
2. African Americans—Civil rights—History—20th century—Juvenile literature.
3. Race discrimination—Law and legislation—United States—History—
20th century—Juvenile literature. 4. Race discrimination—United
States—History—20th century—Juvenile literature. 5. United
States—Politics and government—1945–1989—Juvenile literature. I. Title.
KF4757.G65 2010
342.7308'5—dc22
2009032227

Publisher: Michelle Bisson
Art Director: Anahid Hamparian
Series Designer: Sonia Chaghatzbanian
Photo Research by Candlepants Incorporated

Cover Photo: Yoichi Okamoto / Lyndon Baines Johnson Presidential Library
The photographs in this book are used by permission and through the courtesy of:
Getty Images: 6, 36; Time & Life Pictures, 21, 26, 29, 32, 39, 43, 67, 73, 76, 92, 106, 116; Eric Thayer, 81; Timothy A. Clary/AFP, 2–3, 116. AP Images: 12. Library of Congress: 19, 48.
Lyndon Baines Johnson Presidential Library: Yoichi Okamoto, 104.

Printed in Malaysia(T)
1 3 5 6 4 2

# Contents

The signing of the Civil Rights Act of 1964 marked a monumental change in American law and life. President Lyndon B. Johnson, seated, hands a pen to the Reverend Martin Luther King Jr. after signing the bill that the two men worked together to pass.

# The Magna Carta of Civil Rights

On July 2, 1964, President Lyndon B. Johnson signed the Civil Rights Act of 1964 into law. This historic law granted equal rights to black Americans—at least under federal law. The *New York Times* hailed the legislation as "the most far-reaching civil rights law since Reconstruction days," adding that it was the "most sweeping civil rights legislation ever enacted" in America. The passage of the bill marked a major triumph in the monumental struggle by the nation's blacks to end discrimination against people of color. The fact that a southern president—a Texan—had been the force behind the legislation made the victory all the more remarkable.

Southern politicians dominated the opposition to the bill. They portrayed the battle as one of states versus the federal government and made it abundantly clear that they had no intention of ceding states' power without a fight. And fight they did. For three long months, opponents talked night and day, halting work in the Senate and blocking action on the bill. When the speeches finally ended, the nonstop debate broke the record for the longest in the Senate's history. The House of Representatives, where Johnson Democrats held sway, had earlier passed the bill by a wide margin.

Johnson's political strength and that of the bill's proponents, however, ultimately proved unstoppable. Moderate Republicans led by Everett Dirksen joined with the pro-civil rights Democrats to crush the opposition and push the bill through. The final vote in the Senate came on June 19, 1964, with passage assured by a 73 to 27 tally.

The bill's passage was a turning point in black Americans' long fight for equality. It put federal authority behind the effort to end discrimination at the workplace, in public accommodations, and elsewhere. Those who persisted in discriminating against people because of the color of their skin faced federal prosecution. The law united the three branches of government behind the effort that began with the Supreme Court's ruling in *Brown* v. *Board of Education* to secure equal rights for all citizens regardless of race or color. On the job front, it gave women as well as black Americans an equal shot at securing work and winning promotions. It also barred discrimination toward people because of their religion.

Viewed as a "Magna Carta" by some civil rights advocates, the Civil Rights Act of 1964 opened polling booths, classrooms, factories, and restaurants to black Americans. It unlocked the doors of opportunity and required that the Constitution apply to black citizens as well as white. Although the law's enactment did not wipe out opposition to its provisions or eliminate discrimination, it set the stage for a transformation in public policy that would change the face of America.

# Glossary

Here are definitions of common terms used to describe the legislative process:

**amendment to a bill**—A proposal by a representative or a senator to change a bill in some way. Amendments are voted on and debated just as a bill is.

**bill**—A proposed law presented to Congress by a senator or representative. To become a law, a bill must be approved by both the House of Representatives and the Senate and be signed by the president. A bill can become a law without the president's signature if Congress overrides a presidential veto. *See veto for additional information.*

**cloture**—A vote to stop a filibuster. During the time of the Civil Rights Act of 1964, a vote by two thirds of the senators present was required to end debate. That was changed in 1975 to three fifths of those present. *See also filibuster.*

**committee**—A group of senators or representatives assigned to deal with bills related to a specific topic (energy, education, etc.). Committees may be divided into subcommittees that handle certain categories within the overall topic (atomic energy, special education, etc.). The committee reviews bills, holds hearings, collects information, and makes revisions and recommendations to the full House or Senate.

**conference committee**—A meeting of appointees from the Senate and House to work out differences in the versions of a bill passed by both bodies.

**Congress**—The House of Representatives and the Senate.

**discharge petition**—a petition to force a bill out of committee for a vote on the floor. In the House, a discharge petition must be signed by a majority, at least 218 House members, to go into effect. A discharge petition must have at least thirty signatures for it to take effect in the Senate. Once the discharge petition releases the bill from committee, the full House or Senate votes on the bill.

**enacted bill**—A bill that has been passed by both houses and has been signed by the president into law.

**engrossed bill**—The final version of a bill passed by either the Senate or the House of Representatives.

**enrolled bill**—The final version of a bill passed by the Senate and the House of Representatives and awaiting the president's signature.

**filibuster**—A technique in which senators talk nonstop while the Senate is in session to delay or block action on bills they oppose.

**majority leader**—The leader of the political party with the most members in the House and the Senate. In the Senate, the majority leader directs the schedule and oversees daily business. *See also Speaker of the House.*

**markup**—The process during which a congressional committee makes its final changes in a bill before it is reported to the full House or Senate.

**minority leader**—The leader of the political party with the second-largest membership in the Senate or the House of Representatives.

**pocket veto**—The president's refusal to take action on a bill within ten days of the end of a congressional session. If Congress adjourns and the president has not signed a bill, the bill does not become law.

**president of the Senate**—The vice president of the United States, who presides over the Senate and can vote only in the case of a tie.

**president pro tem**—The person who presides over the Senate in the absence of the vice president. The largely ceremonial post usually goes to the most senior member of the majority party.

**quorum**—The number of senators or representatives required on the floor for the House or Senate to vote on an issue. In the Senate, a quorum is fifty-one members (half the membership plus one); the House requires 218 for a quorum (half plus one).

**resolutions**—Proposals that come before the House or Senate for a vote. They address the internal workings of Congress or a "sense of Congress," an opinion on a subject of interest. Unlike bills, resolutions are not usually signed by the president and do not become law. Joint resolutions—those passed by both houses at the same time—may become law if the president signs them or if Congress overrides a presidential veto.

**segregationist**—Someone who favors separation of people based on race, color, religion, or other factor, generally resulting in discriminatory treatment of one group.

**Speaker of the House**—The presiding officer and most powerful member of the House of Representatives, who administers the business of the House. The speaker is next in line for the presidency should the president and vice president die or be unable to do the job.

**sponsor**—A senator or representative who signs on as a supporter of a bill. Bills may have one or more sponsors. The chief sponsor is the one who introduces a bill to Congress.

**veto**—The refusal by the president to sign a bill into law. Congress can override the veto with a two-thirds vote, and the bill then becomes law without the president's signature. *See also pocket veto.*

**whip**—The assistant to the leaders of the Democratic and Republican parties in the House and the Senate. The whip's primary assignment is to round up votes for bills of importance to the party.

A black woman watches in fear as members of the Ku Klux Klan walk unobstructed in downtown Montgomery, Alabama, preparing for a cross-burning on the night of November 24, 1956, in response to an almost yearlong boycott of the segregated city buses.

## CHAPTER ONE

# Growing Up Black

Black Americans living in the South in the 1950s and 1960s faced daily indignities. Glennon Threatt, who later became an attorney, recalled his life as a black youngster in Birmingham, Alabama. He could shop in downtown stores, but he was not allowed to try on clothes there because white customers would not buy clothing that a black shopper had worn. Most stores had three restrooms, one for white men, one for white women, and one for people with dark skin, the "colored" restroom, shared by men and women. As a black teen, Threatt could not sit down to eat at a store's lunch counter. If he had, he would have faced arrest. A storekeeper who served him would have been arrested as well, because it was against the law for blacks and whites to eat together in a public place in many areas of the South.

When Threatt went to the movies, he paid for his ticket at the booth with everyone else, but then he and his black friends had to enter through a door in the back and sit in the balcony. Whites occupied the seats on the first floor. Some theaters had separate showings for blacks and whites. When he boarded a public bus, Threatt had to find a seat in the back. If he was thirsty, he had to look for a "colored" water fountain to get a drink. Blacks were not allowed in public swimming pools with whites. They could not play a game of basketball at the public recreation hall with white players. When black friends from out of town came to visit, they had to stay at private homes or find a hotel that accepted black guests. Black patients had to seek out black doctors and dentists for medical care; many white health-care providers would not treat them.

As a sixth-grader, Threatt was one of three black students to integrate the previously all-white Elyton School in Birmingham. During his first month there, his white classmates refused to speak to him. Some other students spit on him and shouted racial slurs at him. When he sat down to eat at a table in the cafeteria, all the white students stood up and took their trays to other tables. His white teacher received death threats after she agreed to teach the integrated class.

When Threatt's family and other blacks moved to an area of the city that had once been off-limits to them, angry white hoodlums vandalized cars in the neighborhood, threw bricks through windows, and burned a cross in a nearby yard.

## A LEGACY OF SLAVERY AND CIVIL WAR

Beginning in the 1600s, white southern planters developed a lucrative economy based on cotton production and slave labor. Black men, women, and children, kidnapped from their African homelands by slavers to work as captives on the plantations of the South, were considered nothing more than private property. For more than two centuries black slaves labored under white masters in America.

In 1857, four years before the outbreak of the Civil War, U.S. Supreme Court Chief Justice Roger B. Taney delivered the majority opinion in the *Dred Scott* case, which denied a black slave and his wife their freedom. The slaves had asked the Court to free them because they had once lived in states where slavery was banned. The chief justice ruled that blacks were "beings of an inferior order, and altogether unfit to associate with the white race, either in social or political relations, and so far inferior that they had no rights which the white man was bound to respect."

Abraham Lincoln freed the slaves in Confederate states during the Civil War. The Union victory in 1865 and the Thirteenth Amendment ended legal slavery in America. By the end of 1865 all the former Confederate states except Texas and Mississippi had ratified the amendment, which abolished slavery in the United States. It became law in December 1865. Texas ratified the amendment in 1870; Mississippi voted to ratify it in 1995, but the results were never officially recognized.

The freeing of the slaves did little to erase the prejudices southern whites held toward the Africans they had once owned. Many whites continued to regard themselves as a superior race and viewed black men and women as subhuman. These white supremacists resisted attempts by the victorious North to guarantee the rights of citizenship to black Americans.

Shortly after the Civil War, President Lincoln implemented a Reconstruction plan to restore the nation that would allow the southern states to rejoin the Union. Lincoln's plan put the South under federal control but allowed southern states to set up their own government and elect representatives to Congress after one-tenth of the number of voters

# Amendments

**Amendment 13**
Section 1. Neither slavery nor involuntary servitude, except as a punishment for crime where of the party shall have been duly convicted, shall exist within the United States, or any place subject to their jurisdiction.

Section 2. Congress shall have the power to enforce this article by appropriate legislation.

**Amendment 14**
Section 1. All persons born or naturalized in the United States, and subject to the jurisdiction thereof, are citizens of the United States and of the State wherein they reside. No State shall make or enforce any law which shall abridge the privileges or immunities of citizens of the United States; nor shall any State deprive any person of life, liberty, or property, without due process of law; nor deny to any person within its jurisdiction the equal protection of the laws.

**Amendment 15**
Section 1. The right of citizens of the United States to vote shall not be denied or abridged by the United States or by any State on account of race, color, or previous condition of servitude.

Section 2. The Congress shall have power to enforce this article by appropriate legislation.

in the last election pledged to be loyal to the United States and obey the antislavery laws. Confederate leaders and military officers were barred from leadership roles in the New South, at least for a time.

After the assassination of President Lincoln in April 1865, Andrew Johnson became president. He adopted a much more lenient Reconstruction plan for the South. He allowed the southern states to run their own affairs again, pardoned the wealthy white southerners who had embraced the Confederate cause, and withdrew support for freed blacks. Once they were back in power, the white leaders passed state and local laws that relegated former slaves to a status inferior to that of whites. These black codes, as they were called, prevented blacks from owning land, voting, carrying arms, or moving about freely. Although federal officials revoked the black codes in 1866, these laws served as models for the South's "Jim Crow" laws, which were implemented after the Reconstruction in the 1870s and beyond. Some of the discriminatory laws remained on the books through the mid-1960s. The term *Jim Crow*, from a song of the 1800s made popular by a white showman in blackface, was a derogatory term for blacks used later to refer to segregation. Jim Crow laws set up a system of segregation that separated blacks from whites and discriminated against black Americans in nearly every aspect of their lives.

On a national level, the Radical Republicans, a political group formed before the Civil War to oppose slavery, joined forces with moderate Republicans to pass the Civil Rights Act in 1866. President Andrew Johnson vetoed the bill, but Congress prevailed. Under the legislation, former slaves became full-fledged U.S. citizens with the same rights and privileges as whites. After the 1866 elections, the Radicals gained control of Congress and ordered a much harsher Reconstruction plan. They refused to seat the white leaders who had won election to Congress after Johnson's pardon and put the South under federal control again. They also passed the Fourteenth Amendment, which granted citizenship to "all persons born or naturalized in the United States," including blacks, guaranteed citizens equal protection under the law, and gave Congress the power to enforce its provisions. Tennessee was the only former Confederate state to ratify the amendment, which went into effect in 1868. Congress punished the other southern states by sending federal troops to run affairs in the South. This heightened southern whites' resentment against blacks and their backers in Congress.

For a time during the Reconstruction period, blacks who were, for the first time in U.S. history, legally allowed to vote, cast their ballots, electing several black men to Congress and other posts. Whites, fearful that blacks would seize political control, turned to the Ku Klux Klan and other violent groups. Members of these white supremacist groups lynched, beat, and threatened black citizens, and burned crosses to terrorize them. These tactics prevented blacks from voting and kept them away from public buildings, schools, and other facilities where whites gathered.

In 1869 Radical Republicans in Congress passed the Fifteenth Amendment, giving black men the right to vote and blocking states from restricting voters' rights. The amendment was ratified the following year. The Civil Rights Act of 1875 addressed continuing discrimination against black citizens. It required that public transportation, inns, and other public facilities be open to all regardless of race. Those who were unfairly barred from public facilities had the right to sue, and federal courts had jurisdiction over such cases.

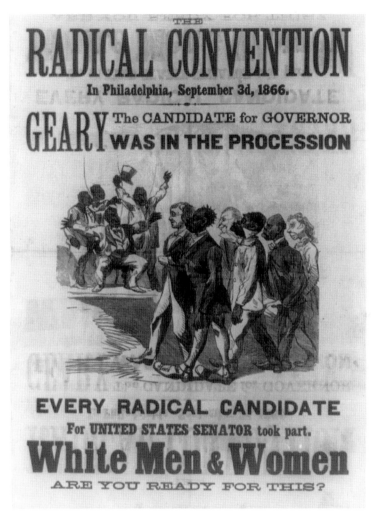

A racist poster attacks Republican gubernatorial candidate John White Geary for his support of black suffrage. The poster pretends to show the convention of Radical Republicans held in 1866, with blacks and whites arm in arm as black men cheer in the background. It was meant to prey on people's fears, and, soon enough, it did.

It was an ambitious piece of legislation, designed to right the wrongs of racial discrimination. Unfortunately, it accomplished little. Courts failed to enforce its provisions, and many states ignored the civil rights laws. Southern states not only dismissed the provisions; they also passed their own laws to keep blacks separate from whites. After Reconstruction ended and the last of the federal troops left the South in 1877, white leaders regained control. From 1881 until 1967, no black Americans served in the Senate. By the end of the 1800s one lone black representative served in the House; and from 1901 to 1929, Congress had no black members. The South would not elect another black American to Congress until 1969, when Missouri's first black representative took a seat in the House.

In many communities, local officials rigged literacy tests or set up other barriers to prevent blacks from voting. Black children were sent to underfunded black-only schools, and employers routinely gave black men and women only menial, low-paying jobs. Theaters, hotels, parks, and restaurants served only white patrons. Often the only blacks allowed in a southern town's nicer public establishments were the cooks, maids, and cleaners who worked there.

In 1883 the U.S. Supreme Court overturned the Civil Rights Act of 1875. The decision, delivered in the *Civil Rights Cases*, ruled that the Fourteenth Amendment applied only to discrimination by states and did not deal with actions by private business owners. The cases, joined as one, came to the Court from five different suits filed after black citizens were barred from public places. Congress would not pass another civil rights law for more than eighty years, until 1957.

A second Supreme Court decision, issued in the 1896 case of *Plessy* v. *Ferguson*, allowed the public railway in Louisiana to continue its segregation policies. The ruling's impact reached far into the next century, upholding a system that gave rise to racial discrimination, hatred, and strife. The Court's decision would stand until 1954, when another

Student protests were an essential ingredient tipping the balance against widespread discrimination. Making the point that segregation defies nature, a student at the all-black Morehouse College stands under a sign proclaiming a tree "a white area."

Supreme Court, the Warren Court, struck it down in *Brown* v. *Board of Education*, the landmark case that barred segregation in the nation's public schools.

Black Americans endured lives marred by injustice and

unequal treatment. Throughout the nation—not just in the South—employers, landlords, and private organizations, including unions, routinely discriminated against black Americans. In many regions of the South, however, segregation was enforced by state and local laws. Even if a sympathetic hotel owner wanted to rent rooms to blacks as well as whites, he could not do so without fear of being arrested himself.

During World War II President Franklin D. Roosevelt, angry over racial unfairness, barred defense contractors from discriminating against black workers. Black soldiers, many serving in segregated units, distinguished themselves on the battlefield. When they returned home, however, they faced the same daily insults and abuses they had before the war. In part to remedy the injustices, President Harry S. Truman ordered the desegregation of the military. By 1953, when the Korean War ended, blacks and whites served together in almost all military branches.

Segregation of the races continued outside the military. Resentment against such treatment finally reached a boiling point beginning in the 1950s. Black leaders and isolated groups of courageous black citizens, sometimes aided by white supporters, had taken stands against discrimination since before the Civil War. But such protests had been crushed by much more powerful forces controlled by whites committed to segregation.

This time, however, the movement took fire under the direction of the Reverend Dr. Martin Luther King Jr. and other capable leaders who inspired both blacks and whites in the push for black equality. King, a Baptist minister from Atlanta, used two effective methods in the campaign for civil rights: nonviolent protest and economic boycotts.

## CHAPTER TWO

# Setting a Precedent

The growing demands for civil rights for black Americans eventually drew the attention of the nation's politicians. In Washington, Republican President Dwight D. Eisenhower and Congress addressed the situation with two civil rights bills. The 1957 Civil Rights Act and its sequel, the 1960 Civil Rights Act, both contained provisions guaranteeing voting rights for black citizens.

## FIRST CIVIL RIGHTS BILL IN EIGHTY-TWO YEARS

Representative Emanuel Celler of New York wrote the 1957 bill and led the effort to pass civil rights legislation in the House. As proposed, the 1957 act gave the U.S. government the authority to overturn state laws that disagreed with the federal civil rights law. It allowed the Justice Department to sue civil rights violators. Previously, citizens had to file their own suits. The proposed bill also gave the U.S. attorney general the power to take action against racial discrimination, instead of waiting for victims to sue. In addition, civil rights cases could be moved from state courts to federal courts, which were generally less biased in such matters.

Although many representatives supported the act, the legislation soon ran into trouble in the House. Southern whites protested that the bill gave the federal government too much power to interfere in states' affairs. Southerners opposed to civil rights held several key positions in the House and Senate at the time. Among these was Representative Howard W. Smith, a Democrat from Virginia, who headed the House Rules Committee. Smith vehemently opposed the civil rights bill. When he encountered a bill he did not like, Smith left his post and retreated to his Virginia farm—a ploy he used to stall the Civil Rights Act of 1957. Without its chairman present, the Rules Committee could take no action on the bill in question.

Texas Senator Lyndon Johnson, in his role as Senate Majority Leader, faced similar resistance from the Senate Judiciary Committee. Senator James Eastland, a Democrat from Mississippi and an ardent segregationist, chaired the committee and refused to release to the full Senate any bill that promoted civil rights for blacks.

Senator J. Strom Thurmond, a Democrat from South Carolina, led opponents of the bill in a filibuster and gave a speech that broke the record as the longest in the Senate's history. Thurmond, who like Eastland was a firm believer in segregation, had written the Southern Manifesto in 1956. The document, signed by nineteen southern senators and hundreds of prominent white men throughout the South, pledged to defy the Supreme Court's 1954 ruling to desegregate the public schools.

Senator Johnson set out to break the filibuster and get the civil rights bill through the Senate. One of the most brilliant

# Filibusters and Cloture

Speakers have made some bizarre orations from the floor of the Senate over the years. In the 1930s, Louisiana's Senator Huey P. Long recited long passages from Shakespeare's *Hamlet* and read his recipes for southern "pot-likkers." He frequently spouted Bible verses and quoted from the U.S. Constitution.

As part of its time-honored traditions, the Senate allows any member unlimited time to express his or her views. Senators who find themselves on the losing side of an issue have sometimes used that tradition to stop the Senate from voting on matters they oppose. Those who use this technique—called a filibuster—talk nonstop while the Senate is in session so that no other action can be taken. By seizing control of the Senate, those engaged in filibusters have sometimes successfully blocked controversial legislation, even when the majority favored a proposed bill. Originally both the House of Representatives and the Senate allowed members to filibuster. As the nation grew and the House gained more members (set at 435 members in 1910), limits were placed on the time allotted for debate there. The Senate, with only one hundred members, continues the practice.

In 1917 the Senate revised its rules to allow the cloture, or cutting off, of debate by a two-thirds majority vote. Because of the difficulty of gaining a cloture vote, filibustering senators could often force compromises on bills they opposed. During debate on President Dwight D. Eisenhower's 1957 civil rights bill, Senator J. Strom Thurmond made the longest speech in Senate history—a one-man filibuster lasting twenty-four hours and eighteen minutes. The effort won Thurmond and his allies revisions that greatly weakened the bill.

Senator J. Strom Thurmond led the opposition to the civil rights bill with the longest filibuster speech in history. He also served in the Senate until he was one hundred years old (2002), by which time the Civil Rights Act had long become history. Thurmond never completely renounced his opposition to it.

In 1975 the Senate revised its rules to reduce the number of senators required to shut off debate. Under the new rule, three-fifths—or sixty—senators can now end a filibuster.

political operatives of all time and a southerner himself, Johnson had many ties to the segregationist leaders in the South. He had not taken a strong stand on civil rights, but he understood the growing importance of the issue. His goal was to keep the Democratic Party from splitting over the issue. As a prospective candidate for president, he also did not want to risk losing the support of blacks and northerners who favored civil rights.

To win southern support for the bill, Johnson proposed a version that removed civil rights cases from federal control. Instead of putting federal officials and federal courts in charge of civil rights cases, the compromise required victims of discrimination to file suit in state courts, where local juries would decide the cases. To win liberals' support for the southern version of the bill, Johnson tied the 1957 act to construction of a dam in Hells Canyon between Oregon and Idaho that would provide electricity for a large section of the American northwest region.

Congress passed the amended bill, and Eisenhower signed it into law on September 27, 1957, the first civil rights legislation in eighty-two years. The act established a Civil Rights Commission to review violations, but it had little strength to enforce civil rights. Nevertheless, the bill was later hailed as landmark legislation that "broke down the barriers to civil rights legislation." Representative Celler called it "revolutionary" and maintained that its passage "was worth the compromise." Liberal lawmakers, he said, "were pretty jubilant that we had this breakthrough."

## ANOTHER WEAKENED BILL

The response to the civil rights campaign in the segregationist South became increasingly violent in the late 1950s. The

# Reading People

Lyndon Johnson had an uncanny ability to "read" other people. He could quickly determine their feelings about a certain issue. Hubert Humphrey, who later became President Johnson's vice president, said that skill, perhaps more than any other, gave Johnson an edge over other politicians.

> Johnson was like a psychiatrist. Unbelievable man in terms of sizing up people, what they would do, how they would stand under pressure, what their temperament was. This was his genius. He used to tell me many times, "You've got to study every member of this body [the Senate] to know how they're really going to ultimately act. Everything about them, their family, their background, their attitudes, even watch their moods before you even ask them to vote." He was a master of human relations when it came to that Senate.

Johnson once advised aide Walter Jenkins to watch the eyes of other politicians. "No matter what a man is saying to you, it's not as important as what you can read in his eyes. . . . The most important thing he has to say is what he's trying not to say."

**The Ku Klux Klan and other racist groups bombed houses, schools, and churches to scare people who were trying to win their civil rights. Here, agents of the FBI investigate a church bombing. At the time the perpetrators of such crimes almost always got off scot-free.**

Ku Klux Klan, a radical group that believed in the supremacy of the Caucasian race, firebombed black churches and schools in the South. Broadcast on the nightly news, the gruesome images of dead and wounded children elicited sympathy and outrage from viewers everywhere. Reacting to the public's demand that something be done to curb the violence, Eisenhower proposed a second civil rights bill in late 1958. This would eventually become the Civil Rights Act of 1960. As before, the bill drew the ire of white southerners, who resented what they viewed as federal interference.

In the House, Smith delayed consideration of the bill by staying at his Virginia farm instead of returning to the capital. Celler tried to force the bill out of committee by convincing House members to sign a discharge petition. This petition is used when members want to transfer a bill from a committee that is blocking its consideration to the full House for debate. The same technique is used in the Senate. To bring a bill to the full House, a discharge petition must be signed by a majority of the representatives. Celler collected 208 names on his petition—just ten short of the number required for transfer. Because of the broad support for the transfer, Smith allowed the committee to vote on the bill and moved it to the House floor for action.

Sidestepping the Senate Judiciary Committee, Johnson brought the bill before the Senate in February 1960. As expected, southern Democrats responded with a filibuster, blocking action on the bill. Other senators voted to hold sessions twenty-four hours a day in an effort to end the filibuster. That strategy backfired. Supporters of the bill were forced to have fifty-one senators in the chambers at all hours of the day and night in case opponents stopped the debate and called for a vote on the bill. Meanwhile, the senators who led the filibuster had only to keep the debate going, a feat easily carried on by a handful of people while others on the team slept.

In frustration, civil rights proponents called for a cloture vote to end the filibuster. When the matter came to a vote, however, fewer than half of the senators supported the cloture. At the time, two-thirds of the Senate (sixty-seven senators) had to vote for cloture in order to cut off debate (that has since been reduced to three-fifths, or sixty votes). The bill's opponents used the defeat to negotiate an act much like the previous one, without mention of any of the federal powers that Celler and his committee had advocated.

The Civil Rights Act of 1960 continued the work of the Civil Rights Commission and allowed the U.S. attorney general to inspect state and local voting records in federal elections. Like the first bill, however, the 1960 version contained only weak enforcement provisions that did little to further civil rights for black citizens.

Neither the 1957 nor the 1960 civil rights laws, however, resulted in any real change, since local juries were left in charge of deciding cases against violators. White juries in the South almost never convicted officials for violating blacks' civil rights. Southern segregationists in Congress lobbied to keep trial by jury in the bill, while civil rights advocates wanted cases to be decided by federal courts, not local juries.

Civil rights advocates questioned Johnson's commitment to their cause because, although he had marshaled both bills through the Senate, he had weakened the civil rights provisions of the bills to win southern support. Even the passage of such laws signified that change was coming. Congress had recognized the civil rights campaign, even if the first attempts at meeting some of its demands had failed.

Johnson's work on the bills foreshadowed the all-out battle he would direct as president to win passage of the far more sweeping Civil Rights Act of 1964. He and civil rights advocates would use the lessons learned in the earlier debates to win a real victory in 1964. The next bill would prove far more effective in combatting discrimination and enforcing civil rights for black Americans.

John F. Kennedy's choice of Lyndon B. Johnson as his running mate attracted votes from southern states and helped Kennedy win the 1960 presidential election. Civil rights legislation proposed by Kennedy, and later Johnson, served to alienate the South and cost the Democrats southern votes in future elections.

## CHAPTER THREE

# John F. Kennedy and the Civil Rights Campaign

In some ways, television orchestrated the civil rights drama that gripped America in the 1950s and 1960s. For the first time, voters had direct access to news events as they happened. Until then, most people in the United States depended on radio and newspapers for reports on the events of the day. Television brought live broadcasts into viewers' living rooms. American families watched, horrified, as southern police officers beat unarmed and unresisting protesters as they sat at segregated lunch counters or marched peacefully down main streets. The nation's viewers saw mobs spitting on young black children on their way to school and heard the ugly insults hurled at them. The graphic shots of racial hostility moved people to anger. They demanded that politicians stop the violence.

John F. Kennedy won the presidency in 1960 by one of the narrowest margins in U.S. history. The liberal Massachusetts Democrat had chosen Lyndon Johnson as his running mate because of his ties to the South. Johnson delivered his home state of Texas and other southern states. Kennedy knew, however, that the powerful southerners who held key leadership positions in Congress would fight any attempt to push through a strong civil rights bill, just as they had in the past. Virginia Senator Howard W. Smith, a Democratic leader in the South who vehemently opposed civil rights measures, still chaired the powerful House Rules Committee. Wilbur Mills, another southern Democrat, headed the House Ways and Means Committee. In the Senate, segregationist James Eastland controlled the Judiciary Committee. In all, southern Democrats chaired twelve of the House's twenty-one committees and twelve of eighteen committees in the Senate. Kennedy wanted to get their support on tax issues and other measures he was trying to push through Congress before presenting a civil rights bill.

In the meantime, though, Kennedy asked Congress to pass other legislation to deal with some of the inequities black citizens faced. On February 28, 1963, the president urged passage of three bills:

- A voting rights bill that provided for referees to settle voting disputes; expedited lawsuits on voting issues; and, in federal elections, eliminated tests designed to keep blacks from voting.
- A bill to expand the duties of the Civil Rights Commission. The board would provide information, advice, and assistance to other agencies involved in civil rights efforts.
- Legislation to provide federal funds and other assistance to help school districts desegregate their classrooms.

## VIOLENCE ESCALATES

Kennedy's initial plan—to delay the civil rights bill until he won approval from Congress for other measures—soon hit a roadblock in the form of T. Eugene "Bull" Connor, the racist public safety commissioner of Birmingham, Alabama. During five weeks of protest and unrest in Birmingham, Connor and his police force beat black protesters with their nightsticks, knocked down demonstrators with fire hoses, and released attack dogs on men, women, and children. The protesters, many of whom were black teens and young children, picketed city businesses and government buildings that enforced segregation and excluded or discriminated against black citizens.

On May 7 police and firemen used high-pressure fire hoses and an armored car to drive back hundreds of rioting demonstrators in Birmingham. The pressure from the hoses was intense enough to skin bark off trees, according to a *New York Times* report of the incident. Rioters threw bottles and rocks at officials. Fred Shuttlesworth, head of the Alabama Christian Movement for Human Rights, suffered chest injuries when a stream of pressurized water hurled him against the side of a nearby church. Public safety commissioner Connor, who arrived on the scene after the black leader was taken to a local hospital for treatment, was quoted as saying, "I waited a week to see Shuttlesworth get hit with a hose. I'm sorry I missed it."

American families watched their television sets in disgust as the evening news broadcast the violent actions of Connor's police and firefighters. Birmingham's jails and detention homes quickly filled with protesters. Many of those imprisoned were under the age of thirteen; police arrested one girl who was seven; another child taken into custody told reporters she was six. Dr. Martin Luther King Jr. astutely

**The tactics of white segregationists backfired when the nation saw live footage of demonstrators being tear-gassed and beaten—by law enforcement agents.**

predicted that the overflowing jails would "lay the whole issue [of civil rights] before the conscience of the community and the nation."

King's words proved true. The Birmingham riots and the police response captured the nation's attention. Officials and public figures throughout the country denounced the police handling of the situation and pledged support for the protesters' cause of civil rights. New York's state attorney general, Louis J. Lefkowitz, called the Birmingham incident "a terrible outrage." Former baseball star Jackie Robinson, who broke the color barrier in that sport, wired his support of the protesters. In a telegram to President Kennedy, Robinson wrote that "the revolution that is taking place in this country cannot be squelched by police dogs or high power hoses." Robinson joined others in organizing a $100-a-plate dinner held at the Park Sheraton Hotel in New York City to raise money to support the civil rights campaign in the South. Families all across the nation added their voices to the calls for civil rights.

On May 8 the House Judiciary Committee began consideration of a host of bills designed to ease racial tensions and offer black Americans help in securing equality. Kennedy, however, was not yet ready to submit a major civil rights bill to Congress. Instead he called on Americans to take actions on their own to quell the violence and do away with discrimination voluntarily. He met with mayors, merchants, organized labor, and other groups and urged them to eliminate racial barriers.

A week after the Birmingham riots, someone bombed King's house and a motel owned by a black businessman, both in Birmingham. Black activists continued their calls for equality, as people from other parts of the country joined in. As the violence escalated, it soon became obvious that mandatory measures were needed to address discrimination, and those had to come from the federal government. Attorney General Robert F. Kennedy told his brother the president that the nation could wait no longer for a tough civil rights bill. Congress had not even acted on the three mild bills the president had proposed in February.

## BUILDING SUPPORT

President Kennedy knew that he would need broad support from the American people and from Republicans as well as

Democrats to win passage of a civil rights bill. He invited nearly three hundred labor union leaders to a meeting on the issue and talked with civil rights leaders and community groups. W. Willard Wirtz, Secretary of Labor, told the labor group that racial unrest was "the most serious problem that we can possibly face." He saw a solution in more jobs and equal opportunity for black workers. After the meeting, George Meany, president of the AFL–CIO, and other labor leaders pledged their help in ending discrimination in unions and at the workplace.

For two weeks in June, Kennedy met several times with congressional leaders from both parties to hammer out details and gather support for the bill. Senate Minority Leader Everett M. Dirksen of Illinois and Representative Charles A. Halleck of Indiana were among the leading Republicans participating in the bipartisan meetings at the White House. The deep involvement of high-profile Republicans in the bill's preparation was "extraordinary," according to the *New York Times*. "At most," the *Times* reporter wrote, "the opposition party would usually be called in the day before a message was delivered and informed of its contents."

While congressional leaders worked with Kennedy on the proposed legislation, Alabama Governor George C. Wallace was defying a federal court order to open the all-white University of Alabama to black students. On June 11, 1963, President Kennedy put the Alabama National Guard under federal control to enforce the desegregation order. When guardsmen arrived on campus, Wallace, who had been blocking the entrance to the university's main door, stepped aside and allowed two black students to register for classes. That evening Kennedy explained his actions in a televised address to the nation. He used the opportunity to urge Americans to

**The growth of the civil rights movement was met with determined resistance from southern whites who believed vehemently in segregation.**

end discrimination against blacks and to challenge Congress to pass a tough civil rights bill. The civil rights crisis, Kennedy said, was "a matter which concerns this country and what it stands for, and in meeting it I ask the support of all our citizens . . . this nation for all its hopes and all its boasts will not be fully free until all its citizens are free."

Speaking with emotion, Kennedy promised to send a civil rights bill to Congress the following week that would speed school desegregation, open public facilities to black Americans, and enforce civil rights throughout the nation. He noted that Congress was the only branch of government that had not embraced "the proposition that race has no place in American life or law." And he warned that unless Congress acted on a civil rights bill, those being discriminated against would be forced to take matters into their own hands. In the face of Congress's inaction, "their only remedy is the street," the president said.

He noted that the bill needed to include a prohibition against segregation in public facilities. Being denied entrance to hotels, restaurants, and other places because of the color of one's skin was, Kennedy said, "an arbitrary indignity that no American in 1963 should have to endure, but many do."

Kennedy issued a passionate plea that black Americans be treated equally. "We face a moral crisis as a country and a people," he said. "It cannot be met by repressive police action. It cannot be left to increased demonstrations in the streets. It cannot be quieted by token moves or talk. It is a time to act in the Congress, in your state, and local legislative body, and above all, in all of our daily lives." He concluded, "A great change is at hand and our task, our obligation is to make that revolution, that change, peaceful and constructive for all."

## "TOO LITTLE, TOO LATE"

Just a few hours after Kennedy's telecast, a white supremacist shot and killed Medgar W. Evers, director of the Mississippi chapter of the National Association for the Advancement of Colored People (NAACP), as the black leader stood in his driveway. The assassination of the thirty-seven-year-old civil rights activist triggered protests and inspired many thousands of Americans to join the fight for civil rights. Thousands thronged the streets of Jackson, Mississippi, during Evers's funeral procession, shouting, "After Medgar, no more fear."

Evers had been scheduled to testify before a House Judiciary subcommittee June 13 on the racial unrest in Mississippi. Clarence Mitchell, representing the NAACP, spoke at the hearing after Evers's death. "He is dead," Mitchell said of Evers, "because the Government of the United States follows a policy of too little and too late in safeguarding the civil rights of colored citizens in the South."

While President Kennedy struggled to put together a strong civil rights package that would win enough support to pass Congress, lawmakers were preparing their own bills to address the issue. Senator Harrison A. Williams Jr., a Democrat from New Jersey, proposed creation of local mediation panels to negotiate solutions to racial disputes. Based on a similar plan proposed by Lyndon Johnson in 1959, the bill would have established a federal agency to oversee the local panels. Johnson had argued that similar mediation boards had for decades resolved labor issues. Williams's bill never went beyond the Senate Judiciary Committee. His proposal received initial support, but some proponents of a tough civil rights bill favored measures that enforced desegregation rather than relying on voluntary mediation.

As nonviolent civil rights workers organized sit-ins at segregated lunch counters, some merchants closed their counters rather than serve non-white customers.

## CHAPTER FOUR

# The Civil Rights Act of 1963

On June 19, 1963, President John F. Kennedy sent his civil rights proposals to Congress. Senate Majority Leader Mike Mansfield would introduce the bill in the Senate, while Representative Emanuel Celler would bring it to the House. Though not as tough as some civil rights advocates would have liked, the bill—titled the Civil Rights Act of 1963—nevertheless offered strong action against discrimination. It banned segregation and discrimination in the workplace and in public accommodations and opened public pools, hotels, restaurants, and other facilities to blacks. Under the bill's provisions, communities and states that continued to discriminate against blacks stood to lose millions in federal funds.

"The time has come," Kennedy said in a lengthy written message to Congress, "for the Congress of the United States to join with the executive and judicial branches in making it clear to all that race has no place in American life or law." The president said the Civil Rights Act would "go far toward providing reasonable men with reasonable means" to deal with the racial strife plaguing the nation.

Although primarily introduced to quell the protests of black Americans, the legislation barred discrimination based on "race, color, religion, or national origin."

The most controversial part of the complex bill outlawed segregation at hotels, restaurants, amusement parks, recreation facilities, stores, and other establishments open to the public. Other sections of the bill asked Congress to:

- give the attorney general authority to sue schools that had not yet desegregated;
- enable the federal government to eliminate discrimination from federal jobs and federal programs;
- set up the Community Relations Service, an agency created to mediate local racial disputes;
- allow the withdrawal of federal funds from programs and activities that permitted racial discrimination.

Kennedy warned that if Congress did not pass a strong civil rights measure, the nation would face "continued, if not increased, racial strife—causing the leadership on both sides to pass from the hands of reasonable and responsible men to the purveyors of hate and violence." If that were to happen, Kennedy said, it would set back the nation's economic and social advances and weaken "the respect with which the rest of the world regards us."

The president asked for calm among blacks and whites while Congress considered the bill. "The Congress," he said, "should have an opportunity to freely work its will." Kennedy urged Congress to stay in session until it had succeeded in enacting "the most responsible, reasonable and urgently needed solutions which should be acceptable to all fair-minded men."

Observers predicted that it would take Congress months to debate the bill. Southern Democrats had already threatened to stage a filibuster in the Senate, which could last for several months. Lawmakers looked ahead to what promised to be "a long, hard summer."

Under Kennedy's bill, businesses open to the public would not be allowed to discriminate if they served out-of-state travelers "to a substantial degree," if a "substantial portion" of their goods came from another state, if any part of the business operations "substantially" involved interstate travel or the movement of goods, or if they were part of an interstate chain. The bill did not specify exact figures or further describe what was meant by "substantial."

The law, if adopted, would dramatically shift the force of the law in the South. At that time, several southern states required people by law to use separate facilities, determined by their race and the color of their skin. Blacks who tried to eat at a "whites-only" lunch counter, for example, were arrested for violating the law. Kennedy's bill sought to invalidate such laws. Business owners who turned away black customers would be the lawbreakers under the new legislation.

Kennedy added a $400 million package of proposals to boost jobs, increase literacy, and expand educational opportunities for those who had suffered from discrimination, along with programs to train the young and the unemployed.

The bill included tough enforcement measures. It allowed individuals as well as the attorney general to file suit against establishments accused of discriminating. Parents or the federal government could also sue schools and colleges to force them to desegregate.

## "EYEBALL TO EYEBALL"

Representative Celler, chair of the Judiciary Committee and a powerful civil rights advocate, gave Kennedy's proposals high marks. "This is the strongest civil rights message ever sent to Congress," Celler said. "The President is seeing eyeball to eyeball with the segregationists, and there is fire in his eye."

Almost immediately, congressional leaders predicted that Kennedy's civil rights bill would pass with few changes. However, most agreed that Congress would not support the provision, outlined in Title II of the bill, that required private business owners to open their facilities to black clientele. Senate Minority Leader Everett Dirksen had already strongly opposed enforced desegregation at privately owned facilities. A watered-down version of the provision—which Senator George D. Aiken, a Republican from Vermont, dubbed the "Mrs. Murphy formula"—might win support, however. Under the formula, only large businesses—those doing $150,000 or $250,000 in annual business—would be required to desegregate their facilities. Smaller businesses, for example "Mrs. Murphy's" rooming house, would be exempt.

All three civil rights bills were submitted in the Senate on the day Kennedy presented his package. Majority Leader Mike Mansfield introduced the president's bill, which was sponsored jointly by Senator Hubert H. Humphrey, the assistant Democratic leader, and Senator Thomas H. Kuchel, the assistant Republican leader. Mansfield and Dirksen sponsored a second bill, which duplicated the president's bill but excluded Title II. Instead, Dirksen called for voluntary community action to stop segregation and relied on federal mediation to settle disputes over discrimination. A third bill, which duplicated the wording in Title II, was introduced by Mansfield and Senator Warren G. Magnuson, Democrat from Washington state and chair of the Commerce Committee. Supporters filed the three bills to ensure that at least some version of the president's civil rights package would be enacted. If senators rejected the Title II provisions, the Senate could still pass a civil rights bill.

The following day, June 20, Representative Celler introduced the president's bill in the House. He said that hearings would begin the following week and predicted that the bill would be ready for consideration by the full House by the end of July. He promised to file a discharge petition if necessary to force Representative Howard W. Smith, chair of the Rules Committee and a bitter foe of the civil rights movement, to release the bill. A strong proponent of the bill, Celler nevertheless said he would ask his committee to modify Title II to apply only to firms doing more than $150,000 annual business.

## DRAWING THE BATTLE LINES

Attorney General Robert F. Kennedy took the lead in rallying public support for the civil rights act. He began his campaign for the bill on June 23, four days after it was introduced in the Senate. During an interview on *Meet the Press*, aired nationally on television and radio, the attorney general strongly supported the section of the bill that would end segregation at restaurants, hotels, and other public establishments. The provision aroused early opposition from white business owners in the South as well as some Republicans and southern Democrats in Congress. "Negroes are insulted daily" when they are refused service at public shops and lunch counters, Kennedy told *Meet the Press*. The administration might consider exempting the smallest shops, he said, but the provision was essential to the civil rights bill.

**After President John F. Kennedy introduced the civil rights bill to Congress, his brother, Attorney General Robert F. Kennedy, took the cause to the streets.**

In Congress, leaders' positions on the bill crossed party lines. Southern conservative Democrats joined conservative Republicans in opposing the bill, while moderate Republicans and northern liberal Democrats worked to pass the legislation.

Longtime civil rights opponent Richard B. Russell, a Democrat from Georgia, prepared to lead the battle against the bill in the Senate. Russell, the powerhouse Senate leader of the Democrats' southern bloc, had once promoted his protégé, Lyndon Johnson, as Senate majority leader. Johnson served in the post until his election as vice president under Kennedy.

On the other side, Senate Majority Leader Mike Mansfield and assistant leader Humphrey, also Democrats, marshaled support for the bill. Joining in the effort was Senator Kuchel of California, Humphrey's Republican counterpart. "With the help of the American people," Kuchel said during a televised interview, "a two-thirds vote of Senators present and voting can be accumulated to cut off a filibuster after it goes on for a matter of weeks." However, Minority Leader Everett M. Dirksen of Illinois, the Senate's top Republican, expressed doubts about the bill. He argued against the provision that would ban segregation in public establishments, asserting that such a requirement would infringe on the rights of property owners. He favored an alternative provision that would make desegregation in such facilities voluntary.

In the House, Celler, chair of the Judiciary Committee, had already proven to be a strong backer of civil rights. Although conservatives outnumbered liberals on the committee, observers believed that Celler would lead a bipartisan majority who would approve the bill.

The one thing everyone agreed on was that the battle over

the civil rights bill promised to be a bitter one. The *New York Times* predicted in June 1963 that the bill's path would be "strewn with parliamentary booby traps, and at the end of the journey in the Senate there may be an epic showdown if the . . . civil rights forces have to break a Southern filibuster."

## UP TO CONGRESS TO RIGHT WRONGS

Committees and subcommittees in the House and Senate do much of the hard work on bills that come before Congress. These committees review the bill, add amendments, make changes, and vote on whether the bill should pass or not. In many cases more than one committee or subcommittee will consider the bill.

Committees often hold hearings on controversial or complex bills. The committee may require experts, government officials, and others to testify on the bill and answer members' questions. Members of the public interested in the bill may also present their views at the hearings. After the committee has discussed and studied the bill, members vote on it. The committee then issues a report on its findings and recommends whether the bill should pass as introduced, should not pass, or should pass as amended. Usually committees table or take no action on bills they do not favor, rather than issuing a negative report. Committee members who disagree with the majority may file separate statements voicing their views.

Only a small percentage of bills are eventually enacted into law. For example, of the 5,815 bills introduced in the House of Representatives from 1999 to 2000, only 957 bills passed. Many of the bills never even make it out of committee.

As the head of the Justice Department, Attorney General Kennedy opened testimony on the civil rights bill, appearing before the House Judiciary Committee's antitrust subcommittee on June 26, 1963. At 10:30 a.m., Kennedy entered the packed hearing room, holding a twenty-five-page explanation of the bill. The room went still, as spectators standing three deep along the walls strained to hear the attorney general's introduction.

Kennedy began by noting that the executive branch and the courts had taken steps to redress the centuries of discrimination against black Americans. He echoed his brother's challenge to Congress to take similar action by passing the civil rights bill. "Now it is clearly up to Congress to bring its strength to bear," he said. "The Constitution provides the means for redressing this inequity. If we do not use those means, we compound the wrong."

The attorney general spent most of the day's session answering questions about the controversial provision that required businesses to open their doors to black customers. Even some lawmakers who favored a ban on segregation questioned whether it should extend to small private businesses. Representative Celler, who chaired the subcommittee as well as the Judiciary Committee, suggested that Congress limit the ban to establishments that did a set amount of business. Such a concession, he noted, might make the law more acceptable to opponents and easier to enforce. Kennedy agreed that the suggestion had "a good deal of merit" and said the administration "would be willing to work something out."

Kennedy's willingness to modify the bill triggered a pointed exchange with Representative John V. Lindsay, a liberal Republican from New York. Lindsay questioned the leadership's commitment to banning segregation in public places. "Do you really want a public accommodations section?" he asked Kennedy. "Rumor is all over Capitol Hill that the leaders have made a deal to scuttle public accommodations." Celler quickly denied involvement in any such scheme. He and others believed Kennedy's concession improved the chances that Congress would pass a strong civil rights bill.

## COMMERCE CLAUSE VERSUS FOURTEENTH AMENDMENT

The debate over public accommodations raised the issue of how best to ensure that the law was constitutional and would not be struck down in court. In drafting the provision that banned segregation by businesses, the administration relied most heavily on the commerce clause in the U.S. Constitution. The clause gives Congress the power to regulate business and trade between states. Supporters of Kennedy's bill argued that the commerce clause gave Congress authority to ban segregation at businesses that had anything at all to do with interstate trade. For example, if a company bought supplies from an out-of-state firm, it would come under the regulations. So, too, would businesses that sold goods shipped from outside state borders or served customers from other states.

Lindsay led a group that wanted to base the new regulation solely on the Fourteenth Amendment's guarantee of "equal protection under the law." Lindsay's supporters believed that action would strengthen the prohibition against segregation and would close up loopholes that might otherwise allow some businesses to avoid the ban.

Kennedy noted that the U.S. Supreme Court, in the *Civil Rights Cases* decided in 1883, had overturned a similar provision in the Civil Rights Act of 1875. In that case, lawyers for Congress had argued that the Fourteenth Amendment's "equal protection" clause gave Congress the power to ban segregation. The Court disagreed. According to the decision, the Fourteenth Amendment applied only to acts by states and had no power over the actions of private individuals or businesses. Although Kennedy agreed with Lindsay that the current Court would probably overturn the 1883 ruling, he said the administration wanted to avoid a lengthy court battle over the bill. "We are going to have enough trouble getting a bill through, and the 14th Amendment would only create problems," he told the members of the committee.

Kennedy pointed out that Congress had used the commerce clause many times before, as a basis for antitrust laws, minimum wage legislation, and other actions.

## SENATE TESTIMONY: "A RIGHT TO COMMIT WRONG"

On July 1 the Senate began its own hearings on the bill. Both the Commerce Committee and the Judiciary Committee would review the bill. Like the House committee, the Senate Commerce Committee called Attorney General Kennedy as its first witness. The committee would address only the public accommodations section of the civil rights legislation—Title II. The administration knew the Senate Judiciary Committee would tie up the bill—with no intention of releasing it to the full Senate—and the bill's supporters wanted a chance to discuss Title II in a committee open to examining all the issues.

The accommodations provision, Kennedy testified, would "eliminate one of the most embittering forms of racial discrimination—the denial of free access to places of public accommodation—restaurants, stores, hotels, lunch counters and other establishments of service or amusement—to a large number of our fellow citizens whose skin is not white."

Kennedy assured the members of the committee that the legislation would not "unjustly infringe on the right of any individual," nor would it cover private homes or clubs. "The only right it will deny," he said, "is the right to discriminate, to embarrass and humiliate millions of our citizens in the pursuit of their daily lives."

Kennedy described the difficulties encountered by black Americans traveling in the South. He noted that many hotels and restaurants were closed to them, that reservations might not be honored once proprietors saw their dark skin, and that they often had to stay at hotels of inferior quality or far from their intended route of travel. Many hotels, he noted, welcomed all white people—even prostitutes, drug dealers, bank robbers, and communists—but turned away black judges, ambassadors, and soldiers.

In addition to the injustice of such a policy, Kennedy cited the damage segregation caused to the nation's economy. Discrimination, he told senators at the committee hearing, "puts an artificial restriction on the market and interferes with the natural flow of merchandise." He noted that the government already required business owners to submit to many regulations. Property owners, too, had to submit to local zoning ordinances, licensing laws, and health and safety regulations. Kennedy argued that many of those who complained that the public accommodations bill infringed on private property rights came from states where the government required segregation. "Surely it is no greater an infringement to compel nondiscrimination than it has been to compel discrimination," Kennedy noted.

The provision did not "seriously or significantly interfere with private property rights," the attorney general said. The only right lost, he added, was "a right to commit wrong." By passing the legislation, Congress would take the problem of discrimination at public accommodations "out of the street and into the courts."

Kennedy went on to define the businesses affected by the bill as those that did "substantial" interstate business. He said the administration had intentionally not limited the bill to large businesses because the discrimination by many small establishments, when added together, also had adverse effects on commerce. He did, however, offer to work with Congress to further define businesses covered under the bill. "But if this is done," he warned, "I believe it should be to sharpen definitions rather than to create loopholes or water down the bill."

In closing, Kennedy pointed to the incidents in Birmingham and other southern cities as proof that a civil rights bill was needed. He likened the protests by black Americans to those decades earlier by miners and other laborers who sought fair working conditions. "This is the lesson of history," Kennedy said. "Any discussion which dwells solely on the demonstrations and not on the causes of those demonstrations is not going to solve anything." For a century, he noted, blacks in America had been required to fulfill the duties of citizenship—obeying laws, paying taxes, fighting and dying in wars—without enjoying the benefits. "In nearly every part of the country," Kennedy said, "[the black American] remains the victim of humiliation and deprivation no white citizens would tolerate." The federal government had to take action, he said, because state and local authorities—who would not even permit blacks to vote—could not be relied on to stop discrimination.

"Thinking Americans" knew that discrimination must stop, and Congress must act to stop it, Kennedy asserted, "not only because [discrimination] is legally insupportable, economically wasteful and socially destructive, but, above all, because it is morally wrong."

## MIXED RESPONSE

After Kennedy's introductory remarks, the Senate committee spent the rest of that day and the next questioning the attorney general about the bill. Senators grilled Kennedy so intensely on the bill's details that he jokingly compared the session to taking the bar exam.

As expected, senators had a mixed response to the bill and to Kennedy's presentation. Minority Leader Dirksen expressed the belief that a public accommodations law barring discrimination would be unenforceable. Senators explored ways to make the bill more acceptable to businesses. One proposal was to include only large businesses in the bill (those with sales of more than $1 million a year). Another would have banned discrimination only in businesses licensed by a state.

The committee postponed further consideration of the bill until after the Fourth of July holiday. Even over the break, however, senators continued to weigh in on the bill. Senator John G. Tower, a Republican from Texas, told a radio audience that the federal government would need a "virtual police state" to enforce desegregation of hotels, restaurants, and other establishments. The bill, he said, would result in "an awful lot of court cases that are really not necessary."

In another broadcast, Senator Allen J. Ellender, a Louisiana Democrat, suggested that lack of ability, not discrimination, was the reason black people were not successful. Irate leaders of African nations had protested the senator's previous remarks that Liberia, Ethiopia, and Haiti, all ruled by black leaders, showed "the greatest evidence of inept government of any I have come across."

Outside of Congress, more than one hundred civic, labor, and religious organizations endorsed the president's bill. The National Education Association (NEA) voted at its annual meeting July 2 to support the legislation. White delegates from Mississippi and Alabama, among eleven southern affiliates that operated separate NEA groups for blacks and whites, shouted loud opposition to the measure during the vote.

Black leaders, while applauding the bill's efforts to stop discrimination, had no intention of discontinuing their own campaign for civil rights. The NAACP declared at its national convention that the bill was "inadequate to meet the minimum demands of the existing situation." The NAACP and six other national organizations devoted to equality for black Americans forged an alliance with civic and religious groups to plan a massive march on Washington, D.C., in August. Meanwhile, other demonstrations occurred in New York City, Philadelphia, Long Island, Baltimore, Chicago, and in many cities in the South. Congress's action—or inaction— might very well "determine whether there is civil strife in both North and South in the months ahead," predicted a *New York Times* editorial. The outcome of the bill could also have "large implications" for the 1964 presidential and congressional elections, the *Times* said.

Members of the Kennedy administration watched the polls closely to gauge the bill's effect on voters. Shortly after Kennedy presented the civil rights bill, a poll showed fewer than 50 percent of the American people thought he was doing a good job as president. A Harris poll conducted in late June gave him higher marks, with 59 percent approving of Kennedy's performance. Either way, though, it was a marked downturn in public opinion, the worst in the two and a half years of Kennedy's presidency. Observers blamed the loss of popularity on Kennedy's push for civil rights, which alienated many whites in the South and some in northern suburbs. Many black Americans, on the other hand, characterized Kennedy's efforts as too little too late. Kennedy's popularity also suffered from his inability to push other programs through Congress. Since January the leadership, controlled by southern Democrats in the Senate, had resisted the president's efforts to win passage of a major tax cut bill and other important initiatives.

Despite the ominous drop in public support, many Democrats believed Kennedy would again gain the people's support once the battle over the civil rights bill ended. An immensely popular president, Kennedy, like most political leaders, had ridden the seesaw of public approval before. After receiving high marks from 72 percent of the American people when he entered office in 1961, Kennedy saw his approval ratings soar to 83 percent after tensions with Cuba escalated that spring. As racial strife flared in mid-1962 and the stock market dipped, public support for the president dropped to a low of 61 percent. Americans strongly approved of Kennedy's conduct during the Cuban Missile Crisis in October 1962, when Kennedy negotiated the withdrawal of Soviet arms from Cuba. His ratings after that incident jumped to 74 percent. His supporters believed that Kennedy would be able to pull out of the current slump in time for the next election.

## CHAPTER FIVE

# A Long, Hard Summer

Back in session after the Fourth of July recess, the Senate Commerce Committee resumed its consideration of Title II with testimony from Burke Marshall, assistant attorney general. Marshall, the head of the Justice Department's Civil Rights Division, told senators that voluntary measures to stop segregation would not work in areas where feelings of white supremacy ran deep. A law was also needed, he said, in situations where one business could take advantage of voluntary efforts by others. "Persuasion will not solve the problem in a locality where all establishments but one want to desegregate, but cannot do so for fear of giving a competitive advantage, in increased white trade, to the one exception," Marshall said. The bill, he noted, was "vitally needed" and had been since the first sit-in was staged in Louisville, Kentucky, in 1871.

A bipartisan group of senators continued to push the administration to abandon the commerce clause and base the bill solely on the Fourteenth Amendment. The Kennedy version, they feared, would open loopholes that allowed businesses that did not do "substantial" interstate commerce to keep discriminating against blacks. They also argued that racial discrimination was primarily a moral issue, not an economic one.

"I believe in this bill because I believe in the dignity of man, not because discrimination impedes our commerce," Senator John O. Pastore, a Rhode Island Democrat, told his colleagues. "I like feeling that what we are dealing with is morality and that morality comes under the 14th Amendment."

Meanwhile, in the House, representatives continued their review of the civil rights bill. While hearings went on, President Kennedy continued to meet with various groups, from unions to businesses and civic clubs to women's organizations, to lobby for the civil rights bill and to ask for help in easing racial tensions.

## SENATE HEARINGS HEAT UP

As Washington heated up in the steamy weather of July and August, tempers flared in the hearing room of the Senate Commerce Committee. Segregationists lodged inflammatory charges against civil rights advocates, evoking angry protests from supportive senators. Senator J. Strom Thurmond from South Carolina led the segregationists' attack with his artfully suggestive questioning.

A committee cannot hold hearings when the full Senate is in session unless committee members unanimously agree to do so. Thurmond withheld his approval to continue hearings beyond the noon bell, which rang when the Senate convened. So each day the committee heard testimony on the civil rights bill only until noon, then adjourned until the following day.

On July 10 Dean Rusk, U.S. Secretary of State, testified that the nation's failure to address racial discrimination had hurt U.S. standing among foreign countries. Thurmond suggested that Rusk, by making such a statement, was siding with the nation's enemy, at that time, the communist-controlled Soviet Union. Rusk bristled at the accusation, and other committee members supported him. The audience clapped when one senator told Rusk that he was one of the committee's "most effective witnesses."

The week ended with testimony from Governor Ross R. Barnett of Mississippi, who spoke against the bill on July 12. The governor sharply criticized President Kennedy for his recent endorsement of civil rights demonstrations. Barnett accused the president and his brother, the attorney general, of aiding a "world communist conspiracy to divide and conquer" the United States by inciting racial unrest. Irate senators chastised the governor for his remarks.

The following Monday, on July 15, Alabama Governor George Wallace charged that John and Robert Kennedy were promoting "a revolution of government against the people." The segregationist governor urged senators to "defeat in its entirety" the civil rights act. He took particular aim at the public accommodations provision, which he said should be labeled "the involuntary servitude act of 1963." And he pledged that Alabama and the South would lead "an all-out effort to defeat any man who supports any feature of the civil rights package."

Thurmond, Wallace, and Barnett all claimed that Martin Luther King Jr. and his allies were communists or were being controlled by communists. Robert Kennedy refuted the charges, saying that the Justice Department had no evidence of any link between the civil rights activists and communists.

The governors also contended that black voters could go to the polls throughout the South. They denied that literacy and other tests were used to discriminate against blacks. In response, the attorney general reported blatant instances of bias. Among the many examples he cited was Tallahatchie County, Mississippi, where 4,329 whites (84 percent) registered to vote, while only five black voters (less than one-tenth of one percent) were recorded. Kennedy produced a stack of statistics to back up his statements.

## ADVOCATES URGE PASSAGE

The Senate committee heard from strong proponents of the bill as well. Franklin D. Roosevelt Jr., acting Secretary of Commerce, testified for the bill on July 23. He argued against making the bill apply only to big businesses. If that happened, Roosevelt said, black customers could still be excluded from 56 percent of variety stores, 76 percent of gasoline stations, 83 percent of eateries, and 98 percent of drinking places. Roosevelt reacted angrily to Thurmond's suggestion that the bill would destroy private property rights, a mark of the communist system. "There is nothing in this bill," Roosevelt replied, "that remotely resembles what the Communists have done."

Ivan Allen Jr., the white mayor of Atlanta, Georgia, told senators on July 26 that the bill's public accommodations provision provided the key to avoiding further racial unrest. Even before becoming mayor, Allen had persuaded business leaders to talk with protesters conducting sit-ins at an Atlanta store. His economic programs and other initiatives, such as desegregating the city's schools, swimming pools, parks, hotels, and restaurants, helped Atlanta escape much of the racial strife rampant in other cities of the South.

Testifying at the president's request, Allen called segregation "slavery's stepchild" and urged Congress to "take action now to assure a greater future for our citizens and our country." He said Atlanta had desegregated public facilities through a combination of court orders and voluntary action. But he said the process would have been easier with a federal law in place that set the standard for local businesses and municipal officials. Allen warned that if Congress did not enact the public accommodations portion of the bill, even cities like Atlanta might "slip backward" and reinstate segregation. If that happened, he predicted a return to "the old turmoil of riots, strife, demonstrations and picketing."

Senator Thurmond subjected Mayor Allen to the same leading questions he had posed to Secretary Rusk. Wouldn't the bill put undue pressure on businesses? Thurmond asked. Allen replied, "It would compel the same rights be given to Negro citizens as to white citizens. . . . Any federal law exercises some compulsion."

Thurmond tried again. Wouldn't the law destroy business in Georgia? he asked. Allen said that it would not. "I don't see any business destroyed," he told the committee.

At that, a furious Senator Pastore of Rhode Island, filling in as committee chairman for the ailing Warren Magnuson, said he would rule Thurmond out of order if he persisted in asking such loaded questions. As chairman, Pastore demanded that all witnesses be "treated with dignity and decorum and not embarrassed beyond the limits of fairness." The audience greeted Pastore's statement with a loud burst of applause. Unrepentant, Thurmond charged that Pastore was trying to gag him.

## LABOR UNIONS DIVIDED

Union leaders joined the chorus of those urging Congress to take immediate action on the bill—some for, some against. AFL–CIO president George Meany continued to lobby unions in his federation to end discriminatory practices. Roy Wilkins, NAACP executive secretary, said Meany's efforts had "some effect," but he told a Senate subcommittee on labor and public welfare, that to blacks denied union membership "the movement seems glacial." Walter Reuther, president of the United Automobile Workers union, warned of another civil war if Congress did not enact Kennedy's bill.

Even so, many unions still shut out qualified black workers, and union support for the civil rights bill was far from unanimous.

James R. Hoffa, president of the International Brotherhood of Teamsters, called Kennedy's bill "a farce and a fake" and accused the administration of trying to "flim-flam the colored people into believing that the civil rights program will provide any jobs." The Teamsters provided the same benefits to black and white workers, although employers often kept blacks in the lowest-paying jobs. Hoffa detested Attorney General Kennedy, who ordered the investigation that led to Hoffa's indictment on corruption and other charges in 1963.

Some union leaders feared that a fair employment provision added to the bill would be used by employers to crush unions. David McDonald, president of the Steelworkers Union, told the Senate subcommittee that the proposal unfairly targeted discrimination in unions. He argued that discrimination should be barred from every workplace, not just those with unions. Otherwise, he said, workers who opposed integration would vote against unions in favor of unionless job sites, where segregation would still be allowed.

## "A THREE-RING SHOW"

While testimony continued at the Senate's Commerce Committee hearing, Senator Sam J. Ervin of North Carolina took over the podium at a hearing before the Senate's Judiciary Committee, which opened testimony on the civil rights legislation on July 16. Ervin read excerpts from the Supreme Court's 1864 decision in the *Milligan* case, which warned of "troublous times," during which the American people and their leaders would "seek by sharp and decisive measures to accomplish ends deemed just and proper." Ervin then announced, "This civil rights bill is the most sharp and decisive measure in this area since the Reconstruction Acts of 1867. It is a drastic assault on the principles of constitutional government and the rights of individuals."

Ervin's words signaled the course the southerners in the Senate would follow in the battle over the civil rights bill. They would use the U.S. Constitution, moral indignation, procedural delays, nineteenth-century Supreme Court decisions, and any other tactics they could employ to weaken civil rights legislation. They particularly wanted to eliminate the public accommodations portion of the legislative package. Several southern senators had already announced their intention of leading a filibuster against the provision. "I expect to fight that proposition until hell freezes over. Then I propose to start fighting on the ice," Senator Russell B. Long, a Democrat from Louisiana, told a radio audience on July 13.

It was clear that the Judiciary Committee would never release any form of civil rights bill for a vote by the full Senate. The Democratic majority, however, had already planned an end-run around the committee. The Commerce Committee, chaired by civil rights proponent Warren Magnuson would release the bill for a Senate vote, or the Senate would deal directly with the version of the bill expected from the House.

By August, it was apparent that Kennedy's civil rights package was not going to be enacted any time soon. Since May the House subcommittee had had twenty-two sessions and had heard testimony from ninety-one witnesses on the civil rights bill. Most had spoken in favor of the legislative package. The Senate's Commerce Committee had also met twenty-two times during which forty-six witnesses had testified. Speakers at those hearings had given both the pros and the cons of a ban on segregation in public places. The Senate Judiciary Committee had met eight times with only Senator Ervin and Attorney General Kennedy sparring so far. A *New York Times* reporter covering the hearings called them "a three-ring show."

## MARCH ON WASHINGTON

Civil rights leaders had been planning a march on Washington for months despite warnings that such a protest at the capital would be counterproductive. "I can assure you that there will be deep resentment," Representative Emanuel Celler cautioned, "and it will prejudice your cause." Members of the Kennedy administration voiced similar concerns. Even Arthur Spingarn, the president of the NAACP, questioned the wisdom of holding the march. He feared such a protest might alienate senators considering the bill.

Despite these warnings, Martin Luther King Jr. and other civil rights leaders pushed forward with their plans for a massive demonstration to be held on August 28. Organizers predicted the March for Jobs and Freedom would attract at least 100,000 participants. Celler warned that a protest in the nation's capital could kill the civil rights bill. The president,

**Senator Sam J. Ervin of North Carolina, was a leader in the fight against the Civil Rights Act. Ervin later became famous as the head of the Watergate Committee, whose hearings led to President Richard Nixon's resignation.**

however, softened his stance on the event. He backed the rally as a valid way to demonstrate support for civil rights—part of a "great American tradition"—but he cautioned against violence by the protesters and by the segregationists who opposed them.

On Wednesday, August 28, 1963, more than 200,000 people thronged the nation's capital to show their support for strong measures to bring civil rights and equality to black Americans. The crowd, a mix of blacks and whites, represented many religions and came from all over the country. It was the largest protest rally ever in Washington's history. As they marched through the streets and assembled on the mall at the base of the Lincoln Memorial, the demonstrators sang freedom songs and young children clapped to the beat of the music. There was no violence. Dr. Martin Luther King Jr. and other leaders of the march met with President Kennedy, who issued a statement praising the demonstration and the marchers' "deep fervor and quiet dignity."

It was King, though, with his vision of a better America, who most inspired those gathered at the National Mall and the millions more watching the event on televisions at home. "I have a dream," he told the hushed crowd. King's deep, sonorous voice carried across the mall with a message of hope. "I have a dream that one day this nation will rise up and live out the true meaning of its creed: 'We hold these truths to be self-evident, that all men are created equal.'" As the crowd roared its approval, King proclaimed:

> I have a dream that my four little children will one day live in a nation where they will not be judged by the color of their skin but by the content of their character.... And when this happens, when we allow freedom ring, when we let it ring from every village and every hamlet, from every state and every city, we will be able to speed up that day when all of God's children, black men and white men, Jews and Gentiles, Protestants and Catholics, will be able to join hands and sing in the words of the old Negro spiritual: "Free at last! Free at last! Thank God almighty, we are free at last."

John Lewis, chairman of the Student Nonviolent Coordinating Committee (SNCC) and later a long-serving congressman, used a more strident tone in his address. Reminding the crowd that "we are involved in a serious social revolution," he denounced the American political system as being controlled by politicians "who build their career on immoral compromising and ally themselves with open forums of political, economic and social exploitation." He warned that if Congress did not enact "meaningful legislation" on civil rights, "the time will come when we will not confine our marching to Washington. We will march through the South, through the streets of Jackson, through the streets of Danville, through the streets of Cambridge, through the streets of Birmingham." Softening his words, he added that the marches would be conducted "with the spirit of love and the spirit of dignity."

The demonstration garnered worldwide coverage. King's words, which would inspire generations of Americans, rekindled the ardor of those working for civil rights. Leaders planned further demonstrations and urged supporters to contact members of Congress with pleas to pass civil rights laws.

Lawmakers held differing views on the effect the march might have on the battle raging in Congress. Most members of Congress had left town for a long Labor Day weekend. Minority Leader Dirksen told reporters the event was "neither an advantage nor a disadvantage" in regards to the civil rights legislation. Senator Philip A. Hart, a Democrat from Michigan, had initially agreed with Dirksen. After the demonstration, however, he changed his mind. "If the spirit captured by news stories and television is correct," he said, "it could produce increased public awareness and public support. This in turn could produce support in Congress."

Others in Congress gave the march mixed reviews. In a televised interview, Senator Thurmond criticized the march as "totally unnecessary" and said blacks had made more progress in America over the past century than in any other country in the world. He reiterated his pledge to fight the legislation with a filibuster if necessary. In the same telecast, Senator Jacob Javits, a Republican from New York, said he believed a majority of Republicans supported the civil rights legislation, as he did.

## STRONGER BILL

In September, after months of hearings, discussion, and review, the subcommittee of the House Judiciary Committee prepared to report the civil rights bill to the full House. During the process, the subcommittee—with a majority of liberals—had made substantial changes in the original bill that expanded civil rights and called for harsher penalties. The subcommittee's version, among other things, gave the federal government broad power to sue those accused of denying the civil rights of others. Such suits would be filed in civil, not criminal, court. Under the Kennedy bill, the federal government was given the power to sue schools to force them to desegregate; the new bill extended the federal suits to cover all public facilities. Citizens who could not get a fair trial in state courts would be allowed to pursue civil rights cases in federal courts.

The modified bill expanded voting rights protections to all elections, not just federal elections. States that prevented citizens from voting would be penalized by losing seats in the House of Representatives.

The new version of the bill also expanded the number of establishments covered by the ban on discrimination. Any business with a state or local permit or license would fall under the antidiscrimination regulations. As a result, almost all businesses would be covered by the bill. Only private clubs and private homes with no more than five rooms for rent would be exempt. The subcommittee also strengthened provisions that barred discrimination in all programs and projects receiving federal funds. Segregated institutions, such as hospitals, would no longer receive aid from the federal government.

Among its most far-reaching revisions were the subcommittee's recommendations to bar discrimination on the job front. The new bill called for fair employment practices that covered most of the nation's businesses and most labor unions. An Equal Employment Opportunity Commission would oversee enforcement of this section of the bill.

Violence interrupted the deliberations in Congress when an explosion rocked the Sixteenth Street Baptist Church in Birmingham, Alabama, killing four young black girls attending Sunday school and injuring more than twenty other people. The fatal bomb blast on September 15, 1963, served as a harsh reminder of the civil rights battles still raging in the South. It was the fourth bombing in black areas of the city in less than a month. The blast occurred five days after three Birmingham schools began admitting black students under court order.

On September 25, as Americans expressed outrage over the most recent bombing, the subcommittee of the House Judiciary Committee released its version of the civil rights bill. Robert Kennedy expressed doubts that the stronger measure would pass Congress. That pitted the Kennedy administration against liberal Democrats and some Republicans, who favored the more comprehensive bill. The split further complicated the push to win approval for the civil rights bill. Before the full House could debate the bill, it had to be approved by the Judiciary Committee and then passed along by the Rules Committee. Chairman Celler predicted that the legislation could be delayed several more months while committee members tried to reach agreement on its various provisions.

## COMPROMISE BILL

The House leaders of both parties worked with members of the administration throughout the fall to forge a compromise bill. Lawrence F. O'Brien, who served as President Kennedy's liaison with Congress, said later that liberals' refusal to support anything but "the strongest possible civil rights bill" almost killed the legislation before it even reached the House. Finally, on October 29, the House Judiciary Committee approved a revised civil rights bill. The bipartisan measure barred discrimination against blacks in the workforce, set up a fair employment practices commission, banned segregation in hotels and restaurants and other public establishments, supported school desegregation, and strengthened voting rights for blacks. The revised version modified some sections and gave states more control. A major change gave local communities and states the right to have a court review decisions to cut federal funds from programs that discriminated on the basis of race, national origin, or religion.

The revised bill's nine sections addressed the following:

- Voting rights. The bill barred subjective literacy tests and other biased exams used to prevent blacks from voting. Those with at least a sixth-grade education were considered literate for voting purposes. The compromise version—as well as the original Kennedy bill—applied only to federal elections. Under the revised bill, special three-judge courts would decide suits brought by the Justice Department against violators of voting rights. The subcommittee bill would have allowed blacks to quickly bring their own suits to trial.

- Desegregation of public establishments. The revised bill retained most of the provisions of the

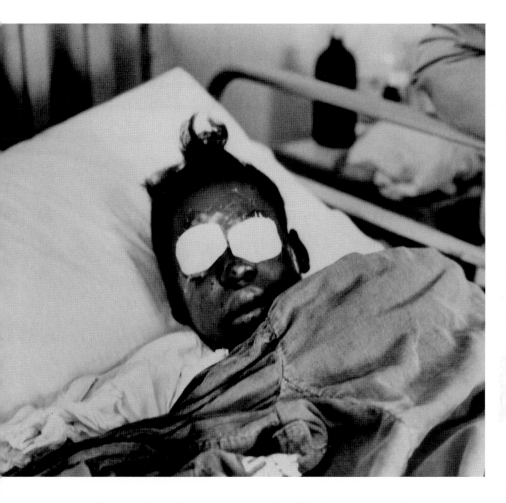

**Sarah Jean Collins was blinded by the explosion that killed her sister and three other girls in a Birmingham church.**

original public accommodations section. Under the new version, rooming houses occupied by the owner and those with no more than five rooms for rent would be exempt. The ban on segregation also did not apply to retail stores not involved in interstate commerce.

73

- Justice Department lawsuits. The new bill allowed the Justice Department to file suit to force desegregation at publicly owned facilities. It also gave individuals the right to sue when denied equal protection under the law "on account of race, color, religion or national origin." The subcommittee had originally proposed giving the attorney general the power to sue those who deprived others of equal protection, but that provision was rejected as too broad.
- School desegregation. The new bill retained provisions that awarded federal funds to school districts taking steps to desegregate. It omitted a section that would have also provided funds to northern schools that took action to balance the numbers of black and white students.
- Civil Rights Commission. Under the revisions, the commission would be a permanent entity with broad duties. Kennedy had asked that the commission be extended for four years in his bill.
- Antidiscrimination in federal programs. Programs receiving federal funds would be prohibited from discriminating against minorities, although federal funds would not automatically be withdrawn.
- Fair employment. Unions and firms that did interstate business and employed at least twenty-five workers would not be allowed to discriminate. Under the new bill, a fair employment practices commission would review complaints and could file suit; cases would be settled by a court.
- Voting statistics. The Commerce Department

would be required to collect statistics on the denial of voting rights.

• Court appeals. People could appeal when they were denied requests to transfer civil rights suits from state to federal courts.

Some civil rights proponents criticized the revised bill as being too weak, but other supporters believed that the bipartisan package had a much better chance of passage. President Kennedy praised the committee for crafting a "comprehensive and fair bill." Emphasizing the bipartisan effort that went into creating the compromise, Robert Kennedy gave special credit to House Republican leader Charles A. Halleck and William M. McCulloch, the Judiciary Committee's ranking Republican.

The committee issued its report on the legislation on November 20 and a day later submitted it to the Rules Committee, where Howard W. Smith of Virginia reigned. Political observers predicted another lengthy battle before the bill would be released for debate by the full House.

The next day, on November 22, 1963, Lee Harvey Oswald, a disgruntled self-proclaimed Marxist, gunned down John F. Kennedy as the president rode through Dallas in the backseat of a Lincoln Continental convertible. Kennedy, hit in the neck and the head, died shortly afterward at Parkland Hospital. Two hours after the shooting, U.S. District Court Judge Sarah T. Hughes administered the oath of office to Lyndon Baines Johnson.

Many thought that the assassination of President Kennedy had ended the chance that the civil rights bill would be passed. They couldn't have been more wrong. President Johnson used the full force of his persuasive powers to turn the bill into law.

## CHAPTER SIX

# Lyndon B. Johnson and the Civil Rights Act of 1964

Only five days after assuming the presidency, Lyndon B. Johnson pledged to continue John F. Kennedy's work on civil rights. In a televised address before a joint session of Congress, he assured the nation that he would push for the passage of the Civil Rights Act. "We have talked long enough in this country about equal rights. We have talked for one hundred years or more. It is time now to write the next chapter, and to write it in the books of law," Johnson declared. He urged Congress to "eloquently honor President Kennedy's memory" by approving "the earliest possible passage of the civil rights bill for which he fought so long." During the intense battle that followed, Johnson frequently evoked the nation's fond memories of the assassinated Kennedy to promote the civil rights bill.

Despite Johnson's words, many civil rights advocates doubted that the president—a white southerner with strong ties to segregationist politicians—would fight for the Civil

Rights Act. They could not have been more wrong. No one had better political skills than Johnson. The president used every means available to marshal forces in support of the civil rights bill. Some political analysts have suggested that the bill might never have passed intact without Johnson's expert maneuvering of the legislation through Congress.

Those who served in Congress when Johnson was Senate majority leader and later president acknowledged that he was one of the most skillful—and determined—politicians of the twentieth century. "Any time President Johnson was involved the push was all out," said Representative Wilbur Mills, who served as the powerful Democratic chair of the Ways and Means Committee from 1958 to 1974. "He was a very forceful individual, very much of a mind of what he wanted."

In the book *Lyndon B. Johnson: The Exercise of Power* (1966), authors Rowland Evans and Robert Novak described Johnson's unique—and often effective—method of persuasion, which observers dubbed the Johnson Treatment:

> Its tone could be supplication, accusation, cajolery, exuberance, scorn, tears, complaint, the hint of threat. It was all of these together. It ran the gamut of human emotions. Its velocity was breathtaking, and it was all in one direction. Interjections from the target were rare. Johnson anticipated them before they could be spoken. He moved in close, his face a scant millimeter from his target, his eyes widening and narrowing, his eyebrows rising and falling. From his pockets poured clippings, memos, statistics. Mimicry, humor, and genius of analogy made The Treatment an almost hypnotic experience and rendered the target stunned and helpless.

## MARSHALING THE FORCES

Even with all his skills, Johnson faced the battle of his political life in pushing the civil rights bill through Congress. Almost immediately he began gathering forces for the fight ahead. On November 25, three days after assuming the presidency, Johnson met with Martin Luther King Jr. to reassure the black leader of his support for civil rights. "I want to tell you . . . how worthy I'm going to try to be of all your hopes," Johnson told King. The conversation was secretly recorded by the president on tape at the White House. Johnson acknowledged the difficulties he faced, noting that the House had not yet passed the civil rights bill and that "everybody wanted to go home" for Thanksgiving. But that did not dampen Johnson's determination to pass the civil rights bill. "I'm going to ask the Congress Wednesday to just stay there till they pass 'em all," he told King. "They won't do it, but we'll just keep them there next year until they do, and we just won't give up an inch." After pledging to do his best to win others to the cause, Johnson asked King for his help. "I never needed it more than I do now," he said.

Used to working sixteen-hour days himself and eager to get the civil rights bill and other programs enacted, the president had nothing but disdain for members of Congress who took long vacations over Thanksgiving and Christmas. A day or two of time off should suffice, he believed, with so much at stake. "They're not passing anything now," Johnson said of Congress in a telephone call. "Whether we have justice and equality is pretty damned important."

He used the time to twist arms, cement relations with supporters, and make telephone calls. The day after Thanksgiving he met with Roy Wilkins, NAACP executive director, to ask his help in getting the civil rights legislation passed.

# It Took a Presiden
# to Get it Done

The Civil Rights Act of 1964 made headline news during the 2008 campaign for the Democratic nomination for president. During a television interview on January 7, 2008, candidate Senator Hillary Clinton proclaimed that "It took a president" to get the Civil Rights Act of 1964 passed. Referring to President Lyndon B. Johnson's role in the epic battle to win passage of the landmark legislation, she made the point that the nation needed an experienced president with the determination and ability to put dreams into action— qualities she said made her a better candidate than her then-opponents former senator John Edwards and Senator Barack Obama (who won the presidency that November). In an interview with FOX News political reporter Major Garrett, Clinton said:

> I would point to the fact that Dr. [Martin Luther] King [Jr.]'s dream began to be realized when President Johnson passed the Civil Rights Act of 1964, when he was able to get through Congress something that President Kennedy was hopeful to do, the President before had not even tried, but it took a president to get it done. That dream became a reality, the power of that dream became real in people's lives because we had a president who said we are going to do it, and actually got it accomplished.

Clinton's remarks ignited a firestorm of protest from those who contended she had minimized the role the civil rights leader had played in winning passage for the bill. She later said that she had no intention of slighting King's

Hillary Clinton's remarks about the Civil Rights Act of 1964, although accurate, ignited a firestorm of criticism during the 2008 primary campaign that weakened her candidacy and threatened to undercut her support from African–American voters.

contributions, only of emphasizing the president's role in getting legislation passed.

Further analysis of the issue demonstrated the partnership King and Johnson had forged to pass civil rights legislation. A telephone conversation between King and Johnson

recorded on January 15, 1965, revealed the close coopera-
tion between the two leaders. The two were discussing the
Voting Rights Act being considered by Congress at the time.
King noted that fewer than 40 percent of black Americans
were registered to vote in the five southern states that had
not voted for Johnson during the 1964 presidential election. Both he and the president agreed on the importance of
passing the Voting Rights Act and discussed the strategy they
would follow to accomplish that. The president suggested
that King illustrate the unfairness of voter registration requirements by broadcasting "the worst condition that you
run into in Alabama, Mississippi or Louisiana or South Carolina." Johnson said King should "take that one illustration
and get it on radio, get it on television, get it . . . in the pulpits,
get it in the meetings, get it every place you can. Pretty soon
the fellow that didn't do anything but drive a tractor will say,
'Well, that's not right, that's not fair,' and then that will help
us on what we are going to shove through in the end."

King agreed, commenting that Johnson's strategy was
"exactly right." Congress passed the Voting Rights Act later
that year.

Wilkins later revealed that Johnson asked "if we would do the things required to be done to get it enacted. He said he could not enact it himself."

The president enlisted the aid of the press, church leaders, civil rights activists, Democrats, Republicans, people who owed him a favor, and anyone else who might be of use in the campaign to pass the bill. When House Rules Committee chair Howard W. Smith refused to hold hearings on the bill, Johnson turned to Katharine Graham, publisher of the *Washington Post*. After disarming Graham with his southern charm and agreeing to speak at a press function, Johnson told of his frustration over Smith's tactics and suggested ways the newspaper could help. Smith's response to a request for action on the bill, Johnson said, had been that "I'm out on my farm and I can't have any hearings."

The president told Graham of plans for a discharge petition to force the bill out of Smith's committee. "Every person that doesn't sign that petition," Johnson told Graham, "has got to be fairly regarded as anticivil rights." He speculated that Republicans could be persuaded to support the petition by portraying them as members of the party of Abraham Lincoln and painting anyone who refused to sign as "not a man who believes in giving humanity a fair shake." If the discharge petition succeeded in the House, according to the president, "that would practically break their [opponents'] back in the Senate."

The *Post*, Johnson advised Graham, should run front-page stories every day asking why Smith and his supporters were opposing hearings. "You can tell your editorial board that this rules committee has quietly said they're not going to do anything. Point them up, and have their pictures, and have editorials, and have everything else that is in a dignified way for a hearing on the floor." In early December the *Post* ran several articles that spotlighted Smith's committee and the delays in considering the civil rights bill.

Johnson, an accomplished deal maker from his days in the Senate, put those skills to work in the civil rights campaign. He told Senate minority leader Everett Dirksen in a December telephone conversation that he would appoint William B. Macomber, a Republican, to a post at the State Department. "You want him appointed, Senator?" he asked Dirksen. "All right, he'll be appointed, period." The president talked to the minority leader with the jovial ease he used with everyone. "There are all kinds of Republicans," he said to the Republican leader. "You're my kind." It was one of many conversations he would have with Dirksen, a key player in the civil rights battle. The opposition of southern Democrats required Johnson to win Republican votes for the measure, and Dirksen as the Republican leader influenced a crucial bloc of votes in the Senate.

The president also took steps to demonstrate his strong support for civil rights to the public. In January 1964 he appointed a black man, columnist Carl Rowan, to head the U.S. Information Agency, despite tough opposition from southern Democrats. "I don't want you to cut his guts out because he's a negro," he warned Senator John McClellan, a Democrat from Alabama. Johnson ordered all those in his administration, including his wife, Lady Bird Johnson, not to speak at segregated gatherings. The niece of Senator Richard Russell of Georgia asked the first lady to speak at an event in that state. "I can't have her [Lady Bird] at a segregated meeting," Johnson told Russell, a longtime Democratic crony. "But," the president offered, "if you ever have any integrated," the first lady would be happy to participate.

## PRESSURE FOR HEARINGS

After meeting with Johnson on Tuesday, December 3, House leaders announced their plan to file a discharge petition the following Monday to pry the civil rights bill out of the Rules Committee. The petition had to be signed by 218 House members. Many members of Congress had opposed the use of discharge petitions in the past, so the tactic was rarely successful. These members believed as a matter of principle that Congress should follow the usual route that gave committees control over bills. Nevertheless, the president urged leaders to follow the strategy. He discussed the petition with King as well.

Johnson also enlisted the aid of Lawrence F. O'Brien, who had served as President Kennedy's special assistant for congressional relations and continued in the post for the new administration. O'Brien's assignment was to round up signatures for the petition among House members. Civil rights groups, labor union leaders, and representatives from the nation's churches besieged Congress in an effort to win support for the petition. One House member told a *New York Times* reporter, "I've never seen one [discharge petition effort] before where we've had the President going, and the civil rights groups, and labor, and the church people."

Liberal Republican John Lindsay of New York quickly announced he would sign the document. But the Republican leadership raised bitter objections. They argued that the bill should follow the traditional route and that Smith should be given a chance to hold hearings on the bill. On December 5, Smith, under pressure from all sides, announced he would hold hearings on the bill "reasonably soon in January." The ranking Republican on the committee, Representative Clarence J. Brown of Ohio, clarified that the hearings would begin in early January and that he expected them to last no more than eight or ten days. After delaying for months, Congress had finally set the civil rights bill in motion once more.

Even with the agreement in place, Celler introduced the discharge petition on December 10. As soon as it was filed, 148 House members, including 24 Republicans, signed it—70 short of the number needed to force the bill out of committee.

The legislative body had passed few bills in this first session, and as the year's end approached, a *New York Times* editorial expressed the view that the 88th Congress had displayed "little grounds for optimism" that it would accomplish much. But, the editorial writer speculated, Congress might yet produce a praiseworthy record spurred by the "intense, restless, driving energy" of the new president. In just two weeks on the job, the *Times* noted, Johnson had managed to rouse Congress out of its torpor. "He wants results. And there is good reason to believe that, because of his own particularly favorable political position [a House and a Senate controlled by Democrats] and because of his past experience [as representative, senator, and vice president], he may even get results."

## CHAPTER SEVEN

# Battle for
# Passage

President Lyndon B. Johnson began the
new year as he had ended the last, pushing Congress to take
action on civil rights and other areas. In a hard-hitting state
of the union address on January 8, 1964, Johnson exhort-
ed, "Let this session of Congress be known as the session
which did more for civil rights than the last hundred sessions combined." Republicans joined northern Democrats to
applaud the president's statement that "surely they [whites
and blacks] can work and eat and travel side by side in their
own country." As an adjunct to the civil rights bill, Johnson
introduced a comprehensive package of proposals to promote voting rights, aid the poor, boost educational and job
opportunities, and provide health care for the elderly. The
president urged Congress to address his proposals, which he
dubbed the War on Poverty, promptly and then take a "fair
and final vote."

Reaction to the speech among members of Congress was

generally positive. Southern Democrats, however, continued their opposition to civil rights legislation in the face of
growing support for the bill's passage. Their leader in the
Senate, Richard B. Russell of Georgia, called the civil rights
act "shortsighted and disastrous," but he acknowledged that
the odds in favor of the legislation were "very great." Nevertheless, he pledged that his faction would "tighten our
belts with increased determination to fight the good fight
for reason and the Constitution with every weapon at our
disposal." The major weapon, as everyone knew, would be
a filibuster the likes of which had never been witnessed in
Senate history.

During the first week of the new session, the House Rules
Committee began hearings on the civil rights bill. Dozens of
House members lined up to testify against the legislation,
but observers expected the bill to finally reach the House for
debate by early February.

As legislative review of the matter dragged on, venues
outside the capital had begun to address discrimination
on their own. In Atlanta fourteen major hotels and motels
announced they would begin accepting reservations from
patrons regardless of race. Several public schools throughout the South were quietly desegregating their classrooms.
But policy makers feared that further delays in civil rights
legislation would spark new protests among black activists
and result in more violence.

Johnson and other politicians in both parties knew well that
the fate of the bill—and Congress's response to it—would
have a major impact on the upcoming election in November.
If Congress did not pass the bill, or instead enacted a much-
weakened version, liberals and black voters might turn
away from the Democratic Party, particularly if conservative

southern Democrats seemed to be in control of the party. Senator Russell, noting the pressure on Johnson to win passage of the bill, predicted it would be "three times harder" to defeat the legislation under Johnson than it would have been under Kennedy. "President Kennedy didn't have to pass a strong bill to prove anything on civil rights," Russell said; "President Johnson does."

By the third week in January, a bipartisan group of Rules Committee members were threatening to cut off debate on the bill and force a vote. Knowing he could resist no longer, Chairman Howard W. Smith agreed to end hearings on January 30 on the bill, which he described as "nefarious."

"I have been here long enough to know the facts of life," he told reporters. "This bill is going to have to go to the floor, and it will have to go pretty soon." The Rules Committee approved the bill 11 to 4.

## THE "SEX AMENDMENT"

With the bill's approval from the Rules Committee, civil rights advocates predicted an easy victory in the House. They had not, however, counted on one final volley from Congressman Smith.

Women who had participated in a long and unsuccessful battle for an equal rights amendment eyed the Civil Rights Act as one way to gain equality for themselves as well as for black Americans. Title VII of the bill specifically barred employers from discriminating against workers on the basis of race, color, religion, or national origin. The legislation applied to most jobs, including professional and management positions. Women proposed adding sex to the list of categories that could not be used by employers to discriminate when hiring and promoting workers.

Representative Smith of Virginia, seeing a chance to weaken the civil rights bill, sponsored an amendment to Title VII that would add sex to the list of protected categories. Smith had supported the equal rights amendment (ERA) in the past, but he treated his own amendment with mocking humor. Others followed suit, including several congressmen who strongly supported the civil rights bill. Representative Emanuel Celler, among the leading advocates of the Civil Rights Act, opposed the ERA and noted that women were not a minority in his house and did not need protection. During the debate on Smith's amendment, Celler joked that his household ran harmoniously because "I usually have the last two words, and those words are, 'Yes, dear.'"

Amid the ensuing laughter, Representative Martha Griffiths, the lone woman on the powerful Ways and Means Committee, angrily addressed the wisecracking lawmakers. The congressmen's laughter, the Michigan Democrat noted, proved the point that women were treated as second-class citizens. In the quiet that followed, Griffiths pointed out that without the amendment white women would be placed at the bottom of the heap, with little recourse against discrimination. "If you do not add sex to this bill," Griffiths asserted, "you are going to have white men in one bracket, you are going to try to take colored men and colored women and give them equal employment rights, and down at the bottom of the list is going to be a white woman with no rights at all."

Five of the seven female members of Congress spoke for the amendment. Edith Green, a Democrat from Oregon, criticized the amendment, saying that it would "clutter up" the civil rights bill. Several southern Democrats opposed to the Civil Rights Act also testified for the amendment and voted for it. They hoped the controversial amendment would result in the defeat of the overall bill. But others truly favored the amendment on its own merits. Many of these supporters were northern Republicans, who also were among the strongest proponents of the ERA. After an afternoon of discussion, the House voted 168 to 133 to add the "sex" wording to Title VII.

Even with the controversial amendment in place, the civil rights coalition in the House was strong enough to overcome the opposition. Two days later, on February 10, 1964, in an overwhelming show of support, the House voted 289 to 126 to approve the Civil Rights Act of 1964. The fate of the bill then passed to the Senate.

## SENATE STRATEGY: THE TEAM

As southern Democrats prepared to bury the civil rights bill forever beneath one of the fiercest filibusters in Senate history, a full contingent of political operatives assembled to fight the battle for enactment. President Johnson commanded the team from the White House. Working eighteen hours a day, he targeted senators for heavy-duty lobbying. Members whose votes were crucial were ushered to the White House for personal talks, called on the telephone, and wined and dined at state functions. The president attended special events honoring senators and suggested a number of Democrats who might be considered for the vice presidential slot in the next election.

The first lady visited with senators' wives. She asked several to help her decorate the family quarters in the White House and invited others to social gatherings.

Hubert H. Humphrey, the assistant majority leader, or whip, led the fight on the Senate floor. A liberal Democrat from Minnesota, Humphrey had been an early proponent of civil rights. He focused on getting the bill enacted with the

**Senator Hubert H. Humphrey, long a liberal and a passionate advocate of civil rights, did yeoman service in shepherding the bill through the Senate.**

accommodations provision intact. "If we can lock up forty Democrats or forty-five," he reported to Johnson in February, "well, we're in business."

Assistant Attorney General Nicholas Katzenbach served as Johnson's White House adviser on the battle. With his help, the civil rights team set up a well-organized campaign designed to outlast the promised filibuster and aimed at collecting the votes needed to shut off debate. It would be a waiting game, and the winner would be the side that could hold out the longest. The southerners hoped that Democrats facing the 1964 elections would accept compromises that would gut the bill rather than risk voters' frustration over a do-nothing Senate. On the other side, Johnson's team hoped that lobbyists and the support of the American people would convince enough senators to vote against the filibuster and for the bill.

Usually a Senate bill would be referred to the Judiciary Committee, but its chair, Mississippi Senator James Eastland, had vowed never to allow any civil rights legislation to pass through his committee, a pledge he lived up to. Committee chairs held the power to set the committee's schedule. Eastland used this power when he refused to set hearing dates for previous civil rights bills. He promised to do the same with the Civil Rights Act of 1964.

To get around Eastland, supporters of the bill followed a Senate rule that allowed bills from the House to be placed on the Senate calendar without being referred to committee. On February 26, under pressure from Senate Majority Leader Mike Mansfield, the Senate voted 54 to 37 to allow the full Senate to debate the bill.

All the debate in committees had served as warm-up exercises for the real battle, which would be fought on the floor

of the Senate. On March 26, as soon as the bill was introduced and opened for debate, southern segregationists—as
expected—began a filibuster to prevent senators from voting
on the act. A Senate rule barred committees from scheduling
meetings while the Senate was in session. Since a unanimous
vote was required to suspend the rule, the filibuster effec-
tively halted all work by the Senate. Hearings on appropria-
tion bills, the long-delayed tax bill, and all other business had
to be postponed indefinitely.

Humphrey's workday, however, often extended far beyond
the standard eight hours. He assigned each section of the bill
to a pro-civil rights senator and reported the team's progress
in a newsletter published early each morning. The newsletter kept members of the team informed on all aspects of the
campaign and included a daily schedule of events. Twice a
week Humphrey met with Democratic allies in the Senate,
their staff members, and representatives of the civil rights
movement to reassure them of Johnson's commitment to
pass the bill. He worked closely with the Leadership Conference on Civil Rights, a loose coalition of civil rights activists headed by NAACP lawyer Clarence Mitchell. Humphrey
made sure that enough civil rights senators remained on the
Senate floor to ensure a quorum should the opposition call
for a vote. During this time, Humphrey kept a running tally of
senators who favored shutting off the debate. As the weeks
passed, civil rights proponents began to agitate for a vote.
But Humphrey, well aware that he did not yet have the sixty-
seven votes needed for cloture, urged his allies to be patient.

## WINNING OVER REPUBLICANS

Both opponents and supporters of the bill targeted twenty
to twenty-five uncommitted senators whose main concern

was that the regulations interfered with the property rights of private businesspeople. Most of these, including Minority Leader Dirksen, were Republicans; a few were western Democrats.

A major hurdle to passage of the bill lay in the Republicans' opposition to the public accommodations section of the bill. Both Johnson and Attorney General Robert Kennedy strongly supported the provision, which they regarded as essential to any civil rights bill. Senator Barry Goldwater, likely to be the GOP presidential candidate in November, had already hurled several volleys against the provision. In his most recent attack, he had charged that requiring private businesses to desegregate was unconstitutional. The opposition of Senate Minority Leader Everett Dirksen, however, was the biggest obstacle to enactment of a strong civil rights bill. Though Dirksen supported civil rights, he had expressed serious doubts over the accommodations provision. Without Dirksen's support and that of the Republicans who would follow his lead, Democrats did not have enough votes to cut off the southerners' filibuster.

Humphrey spent a good deal of time meeting with the minority leader, going over the fine points of the bill, and trying to win his support. Both Humphrey and Johnson knew that Dirksen held the key to success and that they had to do whatever they could to win him over. During an interview on *Meet the Press* on March 8, 1964, Humphrey told reporters, "I think Senator Dirksen is a reasonable man. . . . I think that as the debate goes on he'll see that there is reason for what we're trying to do. . . . Senator Dirksen is not only a great senator, he is a great American, and he is going to see the necessity of this legislation."

Johnson was not particularly happy with having to deal

with the additional controversy posed by the sex amendment. In April, however, the president spoke out in favor of the amendment after being urged to do so by Representative Griffiths. Dirksen initially resisted the additional provision, vowing to remove the "sex" category from the bill. He changed his mind after thousands of voters in his home state of Illinois sent telegrams and letters urging that the amendment remain intact. Senator Margaret Chase Smith, a Republican from Maine, also lobbied Dirksen for his support of the amendment.

To persuade uncommitted senators to support the civil rights bill, Johnson and Humphrey worked with Martin Luther King Jr. and other black activists to flood the Senate with lobbyists, including hundreds of religious leaders. The National Council of Churches spent $400,000 lobbying both houses of Congress on behalf of the act. Mail poured in, urging senators to support the civil rights bill. A Harris poll reported in May that 70 percent of Americans favored the bill and an even larger number wanted the Senate to end the filibuster and vote on the legislation. Dirksen appeared to be wavering in his opposition to the accommodations section of the bill, according to religious leaders who visited him.

This was the opportunity Humphrey had been waiting for. He set up another meeting with Dirksen. The two men spent the next several days forging an amended version of the civil rights bill both could support. Dirksen agreed to the ban on discrimination in public accommodations with an exemption for rooming houses occupied by the owner and which rented no more than five rooms. In turn, Humphrey agreed to limit federal lawsuits against violators of the ban to cases where a "pattern or practice" of discrimination could be shown.

Humphrey made several other small concessions, but all the major points of the bill remained untouched. Among the most important was Title VI, the provision allowing the federal government to withhold funds from any program or project that discriminated against people because of their race, skin color, national origin, or religion. Only Title VII, which governed employment, included a mention of discrimination based on sex. Supporters of that provision had battled hard to win that provision. Another battle to include it in other provisions might jeopardize the gains they had made. The Civil Rights Restoration Act of 1987 expanded Title VI and other provisions to cover gender, age, and disability as well as race, religion, color, and national origin.

On May 14, 1964, the Leadership Conference on Civil Rights reviewed the revised Civil Rights Act of 1964 and approved the changes. With civil rights activists and Dirksen on board, Humphrey finally had enough votes to get the bill before the full Senate.

## "AN IDEA WHOSE TIME HAS COME"

On June 10 at 9:51 a.m., Senator Robert C. Byrd, a West Virginia Democrat, ended a fourteen-hour-and-thirteen-minute speech against the bill. He had spoken longer than anyone else in the debate. Spectators filled the galleries. At 10 a.m. Mansfield opened the morning session for the vote on cloture. "The Senate now stands at the crossroads of history, and the time for decision is at hand," he told the expectant crowd. Senator Richard Russell, who had led the charge against the bill, reiterated that the legislation violated constitutional and property rights and denied that it involved a moral issue. Humphrey followed with a few brief words for the supporters of the bill.

At last Dirksen, tired and worn after marathon days of meetings and work on the bill, rose to address his colleagues. "I have had but one purpose," Dirksen said, "and that was the enactment of a good, workable, equitable, practical bill having due regard for the progress made in the civil rights field at the state and local level." Following the twelve-page speech he held before him, the minority leader openly contradicted Russell by asserting that the issue addressed by the bill was "essentially moral in character." The problem of racial discrimination, he said, "must be resolved. It will not go away." Quoting French philosopher Victor Hugo's words, "stronger than all the armies is an idea whose time has come." Dirksen told his fellow senators, "The time has come for equality of opportunity in sharing of government, in education, and in employment. It must not be stayed or denied. It is here!" He concluded with an appeal to the Senate: "We are confronted with a moral issue. Today let us not be found wanting in whatever it takes by way of moral and spiritual substance to face up to the issue and to vote cloture."

Shortly after 11 a.m., Majority Leader Mansfield called for the vote. Opponents had used filibusters eleven times before to successfully kill civil rights bills. This time, though, the outcome would be different. In the hushed chamber, senators on both sides quietly added their tallies as the clerk called names in alphabetical order to record the votes. When John J. Williams, a Republican from Delaware, spoke his "aye," the civil rights forces knew they had won. His was the sixty-seventh vote in favor of cloture. After seventy-five days of debate, seventy-one senators—four more than needed—voted to end the filibuster, the longest in Senate history. On June 19 the Senate voted 73 to 27 to pass the Civil Rights Bill of 1964.

## FINAL HURDLE

Civil rights proponents had one more hurdle to overcome before claiming victory: the House had to approve the Senate version of the bill. Two days after the Senate vote, Johnson called Charles Halleck, House minority leader, to urge him to push Republican members to approve the Senate version of the bill quickly. The president wanted to sign the bill by July 4, ensuring its enactment before Republicans left for their national convention on July 13.

At first Halleck told Johnson he did not think the bill would go through before the convention. The president persisted, using a mix of cajolery, humor, and arm-twisting. "Well do it between now and the Fourth of July, get these things passed," Johnson pressed, adding, "y'all want civil rights as much as we do. I believe it's a nonpartisan bill. I don't think it's a Johnson bill." Unconvinced, Halleck insisted that Johnson would "get all the political advantage" from the bill. Denying Halleck's assertion, Johnson asked, "You wouldn't want to go to your convention without a civil rights bill, would you?"

Halleck responded, "If I had my way, I'd let you folks [Democrats] be fussing with that [blank, blank] thing, before your convention instead of ours." In the end, the Republican leader conceded, "I'm perfectly willing to give you the right to sign that thing on July 1." But he could not resist adding that he thought Johnson was "taking advantage of an Independence Day thing that ain't right." With typical good humor, Johnson denied it, telling Halleck, "I don't know what you're talking about." The conversation ended with Johnson chuckling and referring to himself as "an old Halleck man."

House members took their own steps to assure the bill's passage. Concerned that Howard W. Smith might use his position on the Rules Committee to hold up the revised bill, a group of Republican and Democrat committee members joined forces to wrest control from the anti-civil rights chairman. After voting to accept the Senate's bill, the committee issued a ruling that limited House debate on the legislation to one hour.

On July 2, 1964, the House convened to consider the Senate version of the civil rights bill. As spectators packed the galleries, the Reverend Bernard Braskamp opened the session with a Bible verse engraved on the Liberty Bell: "Proclaim liberty throughout all the land unto all the inhabitants thereof."

During the debate that followed, Georgia Democrat Charles L. Weltner surprised the gathering by announcing his intention to support the bill. In changing his no vote, Representative Weltner became the only southern Democrat to switch positions. His hometown mayor, Ivan Allen Jr. of Atlanta, had testified earlier in favor of the bill. Before casting his vote, Weltner explained his change of heart, noting that "change, swift and certain, is upon us, and we in the South face some difficult decisions. We can offer resistance and defiance, with their harvest of strife and tumult. . . . Or, we can acknowledge this measure as the law of the land. We can accept the verdict of the nation." Weltner urged his fellow Southerners to "move on to the unfinished task of building a new South. We must not remain forever bound to another lost cause." Civil rights proponents, both Republican and Democrat, greeted his remarks with applause. Southern opponents of the bill "sat stunned," according to a *New York Times* report.

Southern hardliners held to the views expressed by Representative Smith, the House Rules Committee chairman. The Virginia congressman charged that the campaign to pass the act had been characterized by the "heedless trampling upon the rights of citizens." Smith, undeterred by defeat, called the

# Civil Rights Act of 1964

**Signed into law July 2, 1964, by President Lyndon B. Johnson**

The official name of the Civil Rights Act of 1964 reflects the long battle over its passage. The seventy-two-word title reads:

> An Act to enforce the constitutional right to vote, to confer jurisdiction upon the district courts of the United States to provide relief against discrimination in public accommodations, to authorize the Attorney General to institute suits to protect constitutional rights in public facilities and public education, to extend the Commission on Civil Rights, to prevent discrimination in federally assisted programs, to establish a Commission on Equal Employment Opportunity, and for other purposes.

The final version of the Act contained eleven segments, or titles. They dealt with the following:

Title I—Made it illegal to apply different standards to citizens registering to vote in order to block certain groups of people from casting their ballots.

Title II—The accommodations section, which required public facilities such as hotels, restaurants, theaters, swimming pools, and parks to open their doors to all patrons regardless of color, race, religion, or national origin. Private clubs and rooming houses with fewer than five rooms were exempt.

Title III—Banned state and local governments from blocking access to public facilities on the basis of race, color, religion, or national origin.

Title IV—Authorized the attorney general to sue public schools that had not complied with the Supreme Court's order to desegregate; also provided technical assistance and federal funds to assist schools in desegregation.

Title V—Reauthorized the Commission on Civil Rights to investigate allegations that citizens' voting rights were being violated because of their race, color, religion, or national origin. The commission, which also was assigned to collect data on incidents in which people were denied the equal protection of the laws, had to report its findings to the president and Congress.

Title VI—Outlawed discrimination on the basis of race, color, or national origin in all government programs and allowed the government to withdraw federal funds from projects that continued to discriminate.

Title VII—Barred employers with twenty-five or more workers and labor unions from discriminating on the basis of race, color, religion, sex, or national origin; created the Equal Employment Opportunity Commission to hear complaints and rule on violations. Cases in which the commission ruled a violation occurred could be referred to the U.S. attorney general for civil suit or action in district court.

Title VIII—Instructed the secretary of commerce to compile voter registration statistics and other voting data in areas identified by the Commission on Civil Rights. Such information was to include the number of voters by race, color, and national origin.

Title IX—Set rules on court appeals and empowered the U.S. attorney general to intervene in court cases involving the denial of rights because of race, color, religion, or national origin if the case was of "general public importance."

Title X—Set up the Community Relations Service, to help settle disputes over discrimination in local communities.

Title XI—Dealt with court proceedings and other miscellaneous legalities.

bill a "monstrous instrument of oppression" that would be inflicted on all the American people. He warned that further demonstrations led by Martin Luther King Jr. would "inevitably . . . be accompanied by bloodshed, violence, strife and bitterness."

At around 2 p.m., the House, as expected, repeated its previous show of support for the bill, voting 289 to 126 for its final passage. Of the House members supporting the bill, 153 were Democrats and 136 were Republicans.

## LIKE THE EMANCIPATION PROCLAMATION

Later that same day, shortly before 7 p.m., President Lyndon B. Johnson signed the Civil Rights Act into law. The president shared the limelight with the key members of the House and Senate involved in the campaign for the bill's passage. Standing before the cameras recording the momentous event in the East Room of the White House were, among others: Republicans Dirksen, Halleck, and two Ohio representatives, Clarence J. Brown, ranking Republican on the House Rules Committee, and William M. McCulloch, ranking Republican on the House Judiciary Committee, who helped draw up the House bill; and Democrats Humphrey and Celler. Speaker of the House John W. McCormack and Carl Hayden, president pro tem of the Senate, also signed the bill during the televised ceremony. After Johnson added his signature to the bill, he presented the first of seventy-five pens to Dirksen and the second pen to Humphrey. Martin Luther King Jr., on hand for the event along with many other civil rights leaders, also received a pen as a memento. King later said of the event, "It was a great moment, something like the signing of the Emancipation Proclamation by Abraham Lincoln."

During a brief address to the nation after the signing, the

**Between them, President Lyndon B. Johnson and civil rights leader Dr. Martin Luther King Jr., made the Civil Rights Act of 1964 a reality.**

president said the new law provided equal treatment for all, as the Constitution, the principles of freedom, and morality dictated. "Those who are equal before God shall now also be equal in the polling booths, in the classrooms, in the factories, and in hotels, restaurants, movie theaters, and other places that provide service to the public," Johnson said. He asked the nation to "eliminate the last vestiges of injustice in America" and called on "every workingman [and] every housewife . . . to bring justice and hope to all our people—and to bring peace to our land." He said the country had come to "a time of testing" that it could not afford to fail. "Let us close the springs of racial poison," he urged. "Let us lay aside irrelevant differences and make our nation whole."

Described by the *New York Times* as "the most sweeping civil rights legislation ever enacted in this country," the law went into effect immediately with the exception of provisions barring discrimination on the job and in unions. Those became effective a year later. The signing marked the end of law-enforced segregation and the beginning of a new era in which racial discrimination was barred by federal law. Both Johnson and Humphrey considered the victory among the greatest achievements of their political careers.

The Civil Rights Act helped in the fight to remove bogus restrictions that had prevented African Americans from being allowed to vote.

## CHAPTER EIGHT

# A Nation for All

The passage of the Civil Rights Act of 1964 and subsequent legislation mandating equal opportunities for minorities had a dramatic effect on American society. The legislation broke new ground in several areas. Titles II and III of the act abolished state laws that had required segregation between blacks and whites for generations and mandated that public facilities open their doors to people of all races. Titles III and IV gave the federal government a central role in enforcing antidiscrimination laws in public facilities and schools. Under the act's provisions, the federal government could sue owners of facilities that discriminated and could take public schools and colleges to court to force them to desegregate. The act's most effective tool, however, turned out to be a carrot rather than a stick. Title VI, which banned discrimination in "any program or activity receiving Federal financial assistance," proved to be the most convincing way to win compliance of the new law. Faced with losing essential federal funds, schools desegregated, businesses with federal contracts set up nondiscriminatory hiring practices, and public projects financed in part by the federal government became accessible to people of all races.

According to civil rights activist and professor Gary Orfield, Title VI worked to desegregate schools where lawsuits and court battles had failed. It had "more impact on American education than any of the Federal education laws of the twentieth century," he wrote. In the decades that followed, the provision ushered in other legislation that used the same technique to force employers, facility owners, and others to eliminate discrimination against a whole host of citizens, from people with disabilities to women to older Americans.

Another groundbreaking provision, Title VII, created the federal Equal Employment Opportunity Commission, whose mission was to eliminate unfair labor practices. For the first time women as well as blacks had federal law behind them when demanding equal treatment on the job.

Other sections of the Civil Rights Act made important inroads in the campaign for civil rights. Title I barred states from administering tests of voters that discriminated against blacks. Under the law, citizens who had passed the sixth grade were exempt from literacy tests required of voters in some states. A year later Congress passed the Voting Rights Act of 1965, which set up much stricter requirements of states in their handling of voters. Title V established the Civil Rights Commission as a permanent body responsible for reviewing violations of the law. Title VIII directed the secretary of commerce to collect data for the Civil Rights Commission on suspected discrimination against would-be voters. Title IX set up procedures for those appealing federal court orders under the civil rights act and allowed the U.S. attorney general to get involved if the case warranted it. The Community Relations Service was established under Title X, designed to help local areas resolve disputes that arose over charges of discrimination.

## FIRST LEGAL TEST

The first legal test of the Civil Rights Act—aimed at Title II's accommodations regulations—came only one day after Johnson signed the bill into law. Lester Maddox, with pistol in hand and backed by supporters wielding ax handles, prevented black diners from entering his Pickrick chicken restaurant in Atlanta, Georgia. Three black students studying for the ministry filed the suit against Maddox after he chased them from his restaurant. The Justice Department joined in the suit to test the new law. A three-judge panel of the federal district court in Atlanta ruled against Maddox. The panel also ruled against an Atlanta motel owner, who claimed the Civil Rights Act should not apply to his establishment, the Heart of Atlanta motel. Moreton Rolleston Jr., representing the motel, appealed the case to the U.S. Supreme Court. It became the test case that established the Civil Rights Act of 1964 as valid.

In oral arguments before the Court in October 1964, Rolleston relied heavily on the 1883 decision in the *Civil Rights Cases* that ruled the federal government had no power to force private businesses to desegregate. Rolleston also contended that the Fourteenth Amendment and the Constitution did not specifically bar racial discrimination by an individual, that Congress had overstepped its powers under the commerce clause, and that the Civil Rights Act of 1964 violated the Fifth and the Thirteenth Amendments. He claimed that by passing the civil rights law, Congress had taken away "the liberty of an individual to run his business as he sees fit in the selection and choice of his customers." If the Court allowed the law to stand, he argued, "there is no limit to Congressional power to appropriate private property and liberty."

Archibald Cox, solicitor general of the United States, argued for Congress in defending the law. He contended that racial discrimination, in addition to creating social and moral problems, seriously impaired interstate trade. "There was ample evidence on which Congress could conclude that the racial practices in hotels and motels and like places did have a very substantial effect upon the movement of people in interstate commerce," he told the justices. Congress's enactment of the law freed interstate commerce "from restraints and burdens," he said. Cox said that only in a world turned upside down would motel owners be viewed as slaves deprived of their liberty by Congress. Even Alice in Wonderland, he said, would be surprised to learn that those operating public facilities were subjected to slavery.

The Court, in a unanimous decision issued on December 14, 1964, rejected the business owner's claims and upheld the constitutionality of the Civil Rights Act of 1964. Writing for the Court, Justice Tom C. Clark declared that the commerce clause of the Constitution gave Congress the power to regulate local businesses if their operation might interfere with interstate commerce. Under that criteria, the Court ruled, Congress could rightly prohibit racial discrimination by motels and other public facilities. The evidence, Clark wrote, showed that barring black patrons did in fact harm interstate commerce. Furthermore, the new law addressed the problem in a reasonable and appropriate way. Having to abide by federal regulations did not deprive owners of public facilities of their liberty or their property, and they had no "right" to select guests as they saw fit, "free from governmental regulation."

The justices also ruled against a Birmingham restaurant, Ollie's Barbecue, that had claimed its business was all local and did not involve interstate commerce. The law still applied to the restaurant, the Court ruled, because it ordered most of its food from out-of-state suppliers.

The decision cleared the way for the Justice Department to begin full-scale efforts to enforce the new law. After the decision, a federal court ruled that Maddox was in contempt for continuing to refuse to serve black patrons and fined him $200 a day. He closed the restaurant on February 7, 1965, rather than serve an integrated clientele. The notoriety from the case, however, gained Maddox a political following. In 1967 the Georgia state legislature named him governor after no candidate won a majority in the general election.

By the time the Supreme Court rendered its decision, many of the eating places and other public facilities in the South had made the transition from whites-only to integrated. Burke Marshall, who headed the Justice Department's Civil Rights Division, noted that the Civil Rights Act had been widely accepted as the law of the land. "Instead of the resistance to change that we had seen in the past," he said, "we have had massive compliance as befits a nation governed by law and a people who respect and comply with the law."

The Supreme Court's ruling finally made it clear that government policy would no longer tolerate blatant discrimination. Various other sections of the act have been the subjects of similar suits, but the law has withstood the legal tests. Beyond the law, however, lay a host of social problems that would continue to plague the nation and hamper efforts to create a society where blacks and whites would truly be treated equally.

## GREAT SOCIETY

President Johnson set out to address many of the issues that burdened America's blacks and the poor of all races and kept them from attaining equality. In January 1965 he introduced a host of programs and legislative initiatives—dubbed the Great Society—designed to reduce poverty, provide decent, affordable housing, and boost educational and job opportunities for the downtrodden. Many of those programs continue into the twenty-first century.

He also urged black leaders to continue their efforts to register blacks to vote. "Much can be done, and must be done, if the potential freedoms affirmed by the Civil Rights Act of 1964 are to be translated into practice and meaningful progress," he wrote to Martin Luther King Jr. shortly after the passage of the civil rights bill. "The most direct responsibility of each citizen is to participate in the affairs of his nation, state and community by exercising his right to vote. Every qualified citizen must register and vote if we are to be worthy of the freedoms we enjoy and hope to obtain." The 1965 Voting Rights Act, which became law on August 6, 1965, required states to do away with literacy tests and other prerequisites that in effect barred blacks and the poor from voting.

## EFFECTS OF CIVIL RIGHTS LAWS

Almost immediately after President Johnson signed the bill into law, the signs that had relegated black patrons to back doors and substandard services came down. Public facilities opened to people of all races. Faced with the withdrawal of needed federal funds, states complied with the law and required businesses under their jurisdiction to do the same. The act's cutoff clause—withdrawing federal funds from programs and institutions that discriminated—had an impact on schools and job sites as well. All-white schools that had resisted desegregation for a decade began opening doors to black students.

The civil rights law also led to the establishment of governmental and educational programs and policies to offer additional help to those who had been discriminated against in the past. Johnson saw this help as a fair way to correct the wrongs of past discrimination. "Freedom is not enough," he told graduating seniors during a commencement speech at Howard University in 1965. "You do not take a person who, for years, has been hobbled by chains and liberate him, bring him to the starting line of a race and then say, 'You are free to compete with all the others,' and still justly believe that you have been completely fair. This is the next and the more profound stage of the battle for civil rights."

The subject of much controversy, these programs opened doors to education and jobs to a wider group of people. Those in groups discriminated against were given preferential treatment to level the playing field for minorities and women. As a result, a growing number of African Americans and women gained access to higher level jobs. In recent times, affirmative action programs have been cut back or modified by U.S. Supreme Court rulings and conservative government policies. Nevertheless, the programs have presented opportunities to millions of blacks and women and have "been a critical element in creating a substantial black middle class and an affluent black society in a single generation," according to Joseph Califano Jr., a Johnson adviser who later headed the Health, Education, and Welfare Department under President Jimmy Carter.

When the Civil Rights Act was signed in 1964, 2 percent or fewer black students in most southern states attended school with white children; only Tennessee and Texas had a higher percentage. By 1967, three years after the law took effect, nearly a quarter of black students in seventeen southern and border states attended integrated schools. Many students continued to attend schools that were exclusively white or black, however, because blacks were excluded from certain neighborhoods and whites left areas where black families resided. The Civil Rights Act of 1968 barred discrimination against blacks who were renting or buying housing. Court-ordered busing in northern cities also addressed the school segregation that developed as the result of housing patterns. At the beginning of the twenty-first century, few public schools have students of only one race. However, about one-third of America's black students attend schools where whites make up only 10 percent of the student body.

"Today's education system is still segregated and in need of major improvements," according to William F. Tate, an education expert at Washington University in St. Louis, Missouri. "Many cities are as segregated now as they were 50 years ago.... We still have a long way to go to ensure quality learning experiences for many students."

The Civil Rights Act of 1964 "indelibly changed life in America," according to the Center for American Progress, a progressive think tank. It spelled the end to "whites-only" water fountains, swimming pools, and restaurants. After the act was passed employers could no longer legally post jobs that excluded female applicants or that specified "no blacks need apply." It became illegal to fire women just because they were pregnant or not to hire them because they had small children. Under the bill's provisions, hospitals, nursing homes, and other health-care institutions were forced to desegregate. The legislation also established the federal Equal Employment

Opportunities Commission and gave those discriminated against a way to seek justice. "The Act was groundbreaking," according to the center, "and [it] has given new hope, relief, and opportunity to countless Americans."

The Civil Rights Act also had a profound effect on the nation's political life. "The fights over the Civil Rights and Voting Rights Acts were transcendent and defining moments that have shaped American politics from that day to this," wrote Michael Oreskes in a *New York Times* article marking the Civil Rights Act's twenty-fifth anniversary. The bitter battle over the law's passage divided the Democratic Party. Southern whites angry at what they saw as their party's betrayal turned to the opposition party, even though many Republicans had also supported civil rights. On the night after signing the civil rights bill, President Johnson sadly predicted the political ramifications of the act. "I think we just delivered the South to the Republican Party for a long time to come," Johnson told his press adviser, Bill Moyers.

His words proved true. Although Johnson won the 1964 election in a landslide, his opponent, Senator Barry Goldwater, received support from the five states of the Deep South (Louisiana, Alabama, Mississippi, Georgia, and South Carolina). They were the only states, along with the senator's home state of Arizona, to vote for the Republican candidate that year. In the years that followed, the South consistently voted for Republicans for president. The only Democrat to win a majority of votes in a presidential election in the South after 1964 was Jimmy Carter, who like Johnson came from a southern state. Another southern Democrat, Bill Clinton, won the presidency in 1992 and 1996, but he failed to win a majority in the South in either election. Barack Obama, in his successful bid for president in 2008, became the first northern

**Though Republican candidate Barry Goldwater lost the 1964 election to a Johnson landslide, he won the South for the Republican Party. With the exception of the 1976 election of Jimmy Carter, Democratic presidential candidates have lost the South ever since. However, support from voters in three southern states (Florida, North Carolina, and Virginia) helped Democrat Barack Obama win the presidential race in 2008.**

Democrat to win in any southern state since Texas went for Humphrey in 1968.

Black voters played a major role in the election of Obama, the nation's first African–American president. Two million more black citizens voted in 2008 than in 2004, and 95 percent of them cast their ballots for Obama.

In the 1950s only 5 percent of the eligible black voters in Mississippi were registered to vote. By 1964, the year the Civil

# "The Door Has Been Opened"

A record number of people—estimates ranged from 1.5 to 2 million—came to Washington, D.C., to witness Barack H. Obama's inauguration on January 20, 2009, as the nation's first African–American president pledged to uphold the Constitution. For many the event marked a milestone they never expected to see in their lifetime.

Obama, forty-seven, served one term as a Democratic senator from Illinois before embarking on his campaign to become the forty-fourth president of the United States. The son of a white mother from Kansas and a Kenyan father, Obama spent his youth in Indonesia and Hawaii. As the Democratic candidate, Obama won 53 percent of the popular vote on election day, capping a remarkable grassroots campaign that called for change and a new direction for the country. The *New York Times* described Obama's victory as "a national catharsis" that swept away "the last racial barrier in American politics."

The sea of faces at the inauguration attested to the broad support for Obama among all Americans, regardless of race, age, gender, or ethnic background. People in wheelchairs, babies swaddled in blankets, girls wearing burkas and Obama ski caps, old hippies, young rappers, families, teens, and middle-aged couples—all came to see their new president take the oath of office. One man pushed his walker for blocks to get to the Mall, where the day's events were broadcast from Jumbotron television screens. Almost everyone wore a button, a hat, a scarf, or a shirt emblazoned with the Obama logo and bought from the local street vendors, who stood all along the route pushing their wares, eager to make their sales before the moment passed.

Despite the cold temperatures, people smiled and joked

with each other, greeting strangers and contributing to their conversations. The first question was "Isn't it a great day?" The second question, "Where are you from?" Answers spanned the globe: Montreal, Kenya, London, Arkansas, Washington, D.C., California, Minnesota, Maine, Georgia. One black man in his sixties smiled broadly as he marveled over the day's events and pondered how much his late parents would have relished Obama's triumph. "The door has been opened," he said.

The audience quieted as Aretha Franklin sang "My Country 'Tis of Thee" seventy years after Marian Anderson delivered the same song in front of the Lincoln Memorial. Anderson had originally planned to sing at nearby Constitution Hall, but at that time the Daughters of the American Revolution (DAR), owners of the building, required all performers to be white and refused permission to let the black singer appear at the group's hall. First Lady Eleanor Roosevelt, who resigned from the DAR in protest, invited Anderson to perform at the Lincoln Memorial instead.

Everyone in the crowd stood up a little straighter as Obama took the oath of office, his hand on the Bible used by Abraham Lincoln during his 1861 inauguration. At the earlier event, Chief Justice Roger Taney—the author of the *Dred Scott* Supreme Court decision that decreed that blacks were "beings of an inferior order" and could never be U.S. citizens—administered the oath to Lincoln.

As the sun shone down on America's new president, the collective joy of millions dispelled those ghosts of history. In the midst of economic crisis and an unpopular war, this inauguration was not about a divided nation, fear, hatred, or even race, but about hope for a better day for America.

This combination image shows Martin Luther King Jr., left, waving to supporters during the 1963 March on Washington and President Barack Obama, right, speaking to the crowd after being sworn in as the nation's forty-fourth president. King's dream of equality ignited the campaign that led to the passage of the Civil Rights Act of 1964 and the end of legal discrimination against black Americans. The act's sweeping effects opened doors for African Americans in all walks of life, including the presidency of the United States.

Rights Act took effect, 6.7 percent of Mississippi's potential black voters had registered. After passage of the Civil Rights Act and the Voting Rights Act of 1965 and a massive effort to register black voters in the South, the number of blacks on Mississippi's voter rolls jumped to 66.5 percent, 5.5 percent higher than the national average. The number of blacks holding office increased dramatically as well, from a few hundred in 1965 to 6,000 in 1994. In 2008 forty-one African Americans served in Congress; a black woman, Condoleezza Rice, was Secretary of State; and Obama became president.

## UNFINISHED BUSINESS

In the twenty-first century, Americans of all races work together, play together, study together, and socialize together in every region of the country. Some people still harbor prejudice against minorities, but laws that encouraged discrimination against black Americans and required segregation have long been banished.

The gains made by black Americans and women in employment, the end of state-sanctioned segregation, and a well-established federal system to fight discrimination are the lasting legacy of the Civil Rights Act. That legacy, however, "is also one of unfulfilled promise," according to the Center for American Progress. "The Civil Rights Act was so brilliantly crafted that it can be applied to a wide variety of injustices—if there is the will to do so."

Civil rights abuses still occur. Police in some areas unfairly target black motorists. Numerous studies have shown that defendants convicted of killing a white victim are more likely to be sentenced to death than when the victim is nonwhite. According to a 2006 research project, African Americans with dark skin and stereotypical "black" looks who are convicted of murdering whites are twice as likely to be sent to death row than are lighter-skinned African–American murderers. While only 12 percent of the U.S. population is black, African Americans make up an estimated 30 to 40 percent of those in jail for violent crimes.

Investigators have uncovered discrimination against blacks in housing, jobs, and other areas in recent times. African Americans continue to be disproportionately the victims of poverty and unemployment. Underfunded, substandard inner-city schools serve predominantly nonwhite students.

Discrimination still haunts other groups as well. Gay

Americans cannot marry in most states or serve openly in the military. Women continue to earn less than their male coworkers for the same work. In 2007 women workers earned an estimated 76 to 81 cents for every dollar paid to male workers. Only 2 percent of the chief executive officers of America's top five hundred companies were women, and women held only 15 percent of the seats on the boards of directors of those companies.

The dedicated men and women who fought so long in the campaign for equal rights have passed the torch to a new generation. "Civil rights," one commentator notes, "remains the unfinished business of America."

# From Bill to Law

**For a proposal to become a federal law, it must go through many steps:**

## In Congress:

1. A bill is proposed by a citizen, a legislator, the president, or another interested party. Most bills originate in the House and then are considered in the Senate.

2. A representative submits the bill to the House (the first reading). A senator submits it to the Senate. The person (or people) who introduces the bill is its main sponsor. Other lawmakers can become sponsors to show support for the bill. Each bill is read three times before the House or the Senate.

3. The bill is assigned a number and referred to the committee(s) and subcommittee(s) dealing with the topic. Each committee adopts its own rules, following guidelines of the House and the Senate. The committee chair controls scheduling for the bill.

4. The committees hold hearings if the bill is controversial or complex. Experts and members of the public may testify. Congress may compel witnesses to testify if they do not do so voluntarily.

5. The committee reviews the bill, discusses it, adds amendments, and makes other changes it deems necessary during markup sessions.

6. The committee votes on whether to support the bill, oppose it, or take no action on it and issues a report on its findings and recommendations.

7. A bill receiving a favorable committee report goes to the Rules Committee to be scheduled for consideration by the full House or Senate.

8. If the committee delays a bill or if the Rules Committee fails to schedule it, House members can sign a discharge motion and call for a vote on the matter. If a majority votes to release the bill from committee, it is scheduled on the calendar as any other bill would be. Senators may vote to discharge the bill from a committee as well. More commonly, though, a senator will add the bill as an amendment to an unrelated bill in order to get it past the committee blocking it. Or a senator can request that a bill be put directly on the Senate calendar, where it will be scheduled for debate. House and Senate members can also vote to suspend the rules and vote directly on a bill. Bills passed in this way must receive support from two thirds of those voting.

9. Members of both houses debate the bill. In the House, a chairperson moderates the discussion and each speaker's time is limited. Senators can speak on the issue for as long as they wish. Senators who want to block the bill may debate for hours in a tactic known as a filibuster. A three-fifths vote of the Senate is required to stop the filibuster (cloture), and talk on the bill is then limited to one hour per senator.

10. Following the debate, the bill is read section by section (the second reading). Members may propose amendments, which are voted on before the final bill comes up for a vote.

11. The full House and Senate then debate the entire bill and those amendments approved previously. Debate continues until a majority of members vote to "move the previous question" or approve a special resolution forcing a vote.

12. A full quorum—at least 218 members in the House, 51 in the Senate—must be present for a vote to be held. A member may request a formal count of members to ensure a quorum is on hand. Absent members are sought when there is no quorum.

13. Before final passage, opponents are given a last chance to propose amendments that alter the bill; the members vote on them.

14. A bill needs approval from a majority of those voting to pass. Members who do not want to take a stand on the issue may choose to abstain (not vote at all) or merely vote present.

15. If the House passes the bill, it goes on to the Senate. By that time, bills often have more than one hundred amendments attached to them. Occasionally, a Senate bill will go to the House.

16. If the bill passes in the same form in both the House and the Senate, it is sent to the clerk to be recorded.

17. If the Senate and the House version differ, the Senate sends the bill to the House with the request that members approve the changes.

18. If the two houses disagree on the changes, the bill may go to conference, where members appointed by the House and the Senate work out a compromise if possible.

19. The House and the Senate vote on the revised bill agreed to in conference. Further amendments may be added and the process repeated if the Senate and the House version of the bill differ.

20. The bill goes to the president for a signature.

## To the President:

1. If the president signs the bill, it becomes law.

2. If the president vetoes the bill, it goes back to Congress, which can override his veto with a two-thirds vote in both houses.

3. If the president takes no action, the bill automatically becomes law after ten days if Congress is still in session.

4. If Congress adjourns and the president has taken no action on the bill within ten days, it does not become law. This is known as a pocket veto.

The time from introduction of the bill to the signing can range from several months to the entire two-year session. If a bill does not win approval during the session, it can be reintroduced in the next Congress, where it will have to go through the entire process again.

# Notes

## Introduction

p. 7, "the most far-reaching civil rights law since Reconstruction days . . . most sweeping civil rights legislation ever enacted," E. W. Kenworthy, "President Signs Civil Rights Bill; Bids All to Back It," *New York Times*, July 3, 1964, 1.

pp. 9–11, "Glossary," CongressLink, Dirksen Congressional Center. www.congress link.org/print_teaching_glossary.htm

## Chapter One

pp. 13–14, "Glennon Threatt . . . separate showings for blacks and whites." Glennon Threatt, interview, June 16, 2005. Interview U-0023. Southern Oral History Program Collection (#4007)http://docsouth.unc.edu/sohp/U-0023/U-0023.html

p. 14, "As a sixth-grader . . . yard." Glennon Threatt, interview, June 16, 2005.

## Chapter Two

p. 24, "When he encountered . . . in question." "The Civil Rights Act of 1960," African Americans.com, www.africanamericans.com/CivilRightsActof1960.htm

pp. 25–26, "Filibusters and Cloture." Steven Calabresi, Testimony before the U.S. Senate's Committee on the Judiciary, May 6, 2003. www.freerepublic.com/focus/ f-news/907801/posts

p. 26, "In 1975 . . . end a filibuster." "Filibuster and Cloture," Secretary of the Senate, United States Senate website, www.senate.gov/artandhistory/history/common/ briefing/Filibuster_Cloture.htm

p. 27, "To win southern . . . northwest region." Ted Gittinger and Allen Fisher, "LBJ Champions the Civil Rights Act of 1964," *Prologue Magazine* 36, no.2, Summer 2004. National Archives website: www.archives.gov/publications/prologue/ 2004/summer/civil-rights-act-1.html

p. 27, "broke down . . . civil rights legislation." George Reedy, oral history interview, LBJ Library archives, 1983, quoted in Gittinger and Fisher, "LBJ Champions The Civil Rights Act," *Prologue.*

p. 27, "revolutionary . . . worth . . . compromise . . . breakthrough." Emanuel Celler, oral history, Gittinger and Fisher, "LBJ Champions The Civil Rights Act," *Prologue.*

p. 28, "Johnson was like a psychiatrist. . . . that Senate." Dan Cohen, *Undefeated: The Life of Hubert H. Humphrey*, Minneapolis, MN: Lerner Publishing Group, 1978.

p. 28, "Johnson once advised . . . trying not to say." Robert Caro, *Master of the Senate: The Years of Lyndon Johnson,* New York: Random House, 2002, 104.

p. 30, "Supporters . . . slept." "The Civil Rights Act of 1960," AfricanAmericans.com, www.africanamericans.com/CivilRightsActof1960.htm

## Chapter Three

p. 34, "Kennedy knew, however, . . . eighteen committees in the Senate." Ted Gittinger and Allen Fisher, "LBJ Champions the Civil Rights Act of 1964," *Prologue Magazine* 36, no. 2, Summer 2004. National Archives website: www.archives.gov/publications/prologue/2004/summer/civil-rights-act-1.html

p. 34, "Kennedy wanted . . . civil rights bill." Gittinger and Fisher, "LBJ Champions the Civil Rights Act," *Prologue.*

p. 35, "I waited . . . I missed it." Claude Sitton, "Rioting Negroes Routed by Police at Birmingham," *New York Times,* May 8, 1963, 1.

p. 36, "lay the whole issue . . . and the nation." Sitton, "Rioting Negroes," *Times.*

p. 38, "extraordinary . . . At most . . . of its contents." Anthony Lewis, "Kennedy Presses G.O.P. to Support Civil Rights Drive, *New York Times,* June 14, 1963, 1.

p. 40, "a matter . . . citizens are free." Tom Wicker, "President in Plea: Asks Help of Citizens to Assure Equality of Rights to All," *New York Times,* June 12, 1963, 1.

p. 40, "the proposition . . . or law. . . . their only remedy . . . the street." Wicker, "President in Plea," *Times.*

p. 40, "an arbitrary indignity . . . but many do." Wicker, "President in Plea," *Times.*

p. 40, "We face a moral . . . constructive for all." Wicker, "President in Plea," *Times.*

p. 41, "After Medgar . . . fear." Melanie Peeples, "The Legacy of Medgar Evers," *All Things Considered*, NPR, June 10, 2003.

p. 41, "He is dead . . . in the South." Anthony Lewis, "Kennedy Presses G.O.P. to Support Civil Rights Drive, *New York Times,* June 14, 1963, 1.

p. 41, "Senator Harrison A. Williams Jr. . . . mediation." Jack Raymond, "Civil Rights Conciliation Is Pressed in Senate Bill," *New York Times,* June 9, 1963, 1.

## Chapter Four

p. 43, "The time . . . life or law." "Text of the President's Message to Congress Calling for Civil Rights Legislation; Outlines Past Requests," *New York Times,* June 20, 1963, 16.

pp. 44–45, "continued . . . violence. . . . the respect . . . regards us. . . . The Congress . . . its will . . . the most responsible . . . fair-minded men." Tom Wicker, "Kennedy Asks Broad Rights Bill as 'Reasonable' Course in Crisis; Calls for Restraint by Negroes," *New York Times,* June 20, 1963, 1.

p. 45, "a long, hard summer," John D. Morris, "Congress Facing a 'Hard Summer' as Logjam Grows, *New York Times,* July 1, 1963, 1.

p. 45, "Under Kennedy's bill . . . meant by substantial," Wicker, "Kennedy Asks Broad Rights Bill," *Times.*

p. 45, "The law, if adopted, . . . under the new legislation." Wicker, "Kennedy Asks Broad Rights Bill," *Times.*

p. 46, "This is the strongest . . . fire in his eye." E. W. Kenworthy, "One Rights Plea Expected to Fail," *New York Times,* June 20, 1963, 1.

p. 47, "'Negroes are insulted' . . . essential . . ." E. W. Kenworthy, "Congress to Open Civil Rights Fight with 2 Hearings," *New York Times,* June 24, 1963, 1.

p. 49, "Russell, the powerhouse . . . under Kennedy." Kenworthy, "Congress to Open Civil Rights Fight," *Times.*

p. 49, "With the help . . . matter of weeks." Kenworthy, "Congress to Open Civil Rights Fight," *Times.*

p. 50, "strewn with. . . Southern filibuster." Kenworthy, "Congress to Open Civil Rights Fight," *Times.*

p. 50, "For example . . . 957 bills passed." The Dirksen Congressional Center, Senate workload, 1947–2000. www.congresslink.org/print_basics_histmats_workload-stats.htm

p. 51, "At 10:30 a.m., Kennedy . . . general's introduction." E. W. Kenworthy, "Robert Kennedy Offers to Modify Civil Rights Bill," *New York Times,* June 27, 1963, 1.

p. 51, "Now it is clearly . . . compound the wrong." "Excerpts From Statement by Robert Kennedy on the Civil Rights Bill," *New York Times,* July 2, 1963, 12.

p. 51, "a good deal . . . work something out." Kenworthy, "Robert Kennedy Offers to Modify Civil Rights Bill," *New York Times,* June 27, 1963, 1.

pp. 51–52, "Do you really . . . scuttle public accommodations." Kenworthy, "Kennedy Offers to Modify Civil Rights," *Times,* June 27, 1963, 1.

p. 53, "We are going . . . create problems." Kenworthy, "Kennedy Offers to Modify Civil Rights," *Times.*

p. 54, "Kennedy described . . . and soldiers." "Excerpts From Statement by Robert Kennedy," *Times.*

p. 54, "puts an artificial . . . merchandise. . . . Surely . . . to compel discrimination." "Excerpts From Statement by Robert Kennedy," *Times.*

pp. 54–55, "The provision . . . 'into the courts.'" "Excerpts From Statement by Robert Kennedy," *Times.*

p. 55, "But if this . . . water down the bill." "Excerpts From Statement by Robert Kennedy," *Times.*

p. 55, "'This is the lesson' . . . to stop discrimination." "Excerpts From Statement by Robert Kennedy," *Times.*

pp. 55–56, "Thinking Americans . . . morally wrong." "Excerpts From Statement by Robert Kennedy," *Times.*

p. 56, "Senators grilled . . . bar exam." E. W. Kenworthy, "Senators Press Robert Kennedy on Rights Plan," *New York Times,* July 2, 1963, 1.

p. 56, "virtual police state" . . . "an awful lot . . . not necessary." Jack Raymond, "Tower Attacks Rights Proposal," *New York Times,* July 7, 1963, 44.

pp. 56–57, "In another broadcast . . . 'come across.'" Raymond, "Tower Attacks Rights Proposal," *Times.*

p. 57, "The National Education . . . the vote," Robert H. Terte, "N.E.A. Endorses Civil Rights Bill," *New York Times*, July 3, 1963, 11.

p. 57, "inadequate to meet . . . situation." Kenworthy, "Two Parties," *Times*.

p. 57, "determine whether . . . large implications." "The Nation: Pressures for Rights," Editorial, *New York Times*, July 7, 1963, E2.

pp. 57–58, "a poll showed . . . important initiatives." Warren Weaver Jr., "At Home: The President's Popularity Seems to Be Slipping," *New York Times*, July 7, 1963, E3.

p. 58, "After receiving . . . next election." Weaver, "At Home," *Times*.

## Chapter Five

p. 59, "Persuasion will not . . . exception." E. W. Kenworthy, "Civil Rights Aide Calls Bill Vital," *New York Times*, July 9, 1963, 1.

p. 60, "I believe in this bill . . . 14th Amendment." E. W. Kenworthy, "Senators Press Rights Bill Shift," *New York Times*, July 10, 1963, 1.

p. 61, "most effective witness." E. W. Kenworthy, "Rusk and Thurmond Clash Coldly Over Civil Rights," *New York Times*, July 11, 1963, 1.

p. 61, "The governor . . . for his remarks." E. W. Kenworthy, "Barnett Charges Kennedys Assist Red Racial Plot," *New York Times*, July 13, 1963, 1.

p. 61, "a revolution . . . the civil rights package." Excerpts from Gov. Wallace's Testimony, *New York Times*, July 16, 1963, 16.

p. 62, "Among the many examples . . . back up his statements." E. W. Kenworthy, "South Seeks to Water Down Civil Rights Bill," Week in Review, *New York Times*, July 21, 1963, 113.

p. 62, "There is . . . Communists have done." E. W. Kenworthy, "Civil Rights Session Enlivened by Flurry of Partisan Sniping," *New York Times*, July 24, 1963, 17.

p. 63, "slavery's stepchild . . . and picketing." E. W. Kenworthy, "Atlanta's Mayor Backs Rights Bill as Help to Cities," *New York Times*, July 27, 1963, 1.

p. 63, "It would compel . . . some compulsion." Kenworthy, "Atlanta's Mayor Backs Rights Bill," *Times*.

p. 63, "I don't see . . . destroyed." Kenworthy, "Atlanta's Mayor Backs Rights Bill," *Times*.

p. 63, "At that . . . gag him." Kenworthy, "Atlanta's Mayor Backs Rights Bill," *Times*.

p. 64, "Roy Wilkins . . . 'glacial.'" Kenworthy, "Atlanta's Mayor Backs Rights Bill," *Times*.

p. 64, "Walter Reuther . . . enact Kennedy's bill." Jack Langguth, "Reuther Foresees a Civil War Unless Rights Program Passes," *New York Times*, July 31, 1963, 13.

p. 64, "James R. Hoffa . . . 'provide any jobs.'" Associated Press, "Hoffa Criticized Bill," *New York Times*, August 23, 1963, 11.

p. 65, "troublous times, . . . just and proper." Chief Justice Salmon P. Chase in *Ex parte Milligan*, quoted in Kenworthy, "South Seeks to Water Down Civil Rights Bill," *Times*.

p. 65, "This civil rights bill . . . rights of individuals." Kenworthy, "South Seeks to Water Down Civil Rights Bill," *Times*.

p. 65, "I expect . . . on the ice." UPI, "2 Senators Vow Rights Filibuster," *Times*.

pp. 65–66, "The Commerce Committee . . . from the House." E. W. Kenworthy, "Rights Bill: The Arguments in Congress," *New York Times*, August 4, 1963, 138.

p. 66, "a three-ring show." Kenworthy, "Atlanta's Mayor Backs Rights Bill," *Times*, July 27, 1963, 1.

p. 66, "I can assure you . . . your cause." Anthony Lewis, "Kennedy Presses G.O.P. to Support Civil Rights Drive, *New York Times*, June 14, 1963, 1.

p. 66, "Even Arthur Spingarn . . . considering the bill." "The Nation: Pressures for Rights," Editorial, *New York Times*, July 7, 1963, E2.

p. 67, "great American tradition." "The Nation: Pressures on Rights," *New York Times*, July 21, 1963, 110.

p. 68, "deep fervor and quiet dignity." E. W. Kenworthy, "200,000 March for Civil Rights in Orderly Washington Rally; President Sees Gain for Negro," *New York Times*, August 29, 1963, 1.

p. 68, "I have a dream" speech. Martin Luther King Jr., quoted in E. W. Kenworthy, "200,000 March," *Times*.

pp. 68–69, "we are involved . . . of dignity." Kenworthy, "200,000 March," *Times*.

p. 69–70, "Most members . . . as he did." Hedrick Smith, "Leaders of March Pledge Widening of Rights Drive," *New York Times*, August 30, 1963, 1.

p. 72, "Lawrence F. O'Brien . . . reached the House." Ted Gittinger and Allen Fisher, "LBJ Champions the Civil Rights Act of 1964," *Prologue Magazine* 36, no. 2, Summer 2004. National Archives website: www.archives.gov/publications/prologue/2004/summer/civil-rights-act-1.html

pp. 72–75, Revised bill's nine sections. "House Unit Votes Bipartisan Plan for Civil Rights," *New York Times*, October 30, 1963, 1.

p. 75, "President Kennedy praised . . . Committee's ranking Republican." "House Unit Votes Bipartisan Plan for Civil Rights," *New York Times*, October 30, 1963, 1.

## Chapter Six

p. 77, "We have talked . . . fought so long." Lyndon B. Johnson, "Address Before a Joint Session of the Congress," November 27, 1963, Lyndon Baines Johnson Library and Museum, www.lbjlib.utexas.edu/johnson/archives.hom/speeches.hom/631127.asp

p. 78, "Any time President Johnson . . . he wanted." Transcript, Wilbur Mills Oral History Interview I, November 2, 1971, by Joe B. Frantz, Internet copy, LBJ Library.

p. 78, "Its tone . . . stunned and helpless." Rowland Evans and Robert Novak, *Lyndon B. Johnson: The Exercise of Power*. New York: New American Library, 1966.

p. 79, "I want to tell you . . . I do now." Lyndon B. Johnson tapes, Phil Ponce, "Caught on Tape," *The Online NewsHour*, PBS, October 14, 1997.

p. 79, "They're not . . . important." Lyndon B. Johnson and Katharine Graham, audiotape number K6312.01 of telephone conversation, December 2, 1963, Miller Center, http://tapes.millercenter.virginia.edu/pages/listen_tapes_lbj_tel.htm

p. 80, "I would point . . . accomplished," Hillary Clinton, interview by Major Garrett, FOX News, January 7, 2008. http://embeds.blogs.foxnews.com/2008/01/07/clinton-talks-tears-with-fox-news/

p. 82, "the worst condition . . . South Carolina"; "take that one . . . in the end"; and "exactly right," Mary Jo Murphy, "The Nation: Phone Call Into History," Week in Review, *New York Times*, January 27, 2008.

p. 83, "if we would . . . enact it himself." Ted Gittinger and Allen Fisher, "LBJ Champions the Civil Rights Act of 1964," *Prologue Magazine* 36, no. 2, Summer 2004. National Archives website: www.archives.gov/publications/prologue/2004/summer/civil-rights-act-1.html

p. 83, "I'm out . . . any hearings." Johnson and Graham, audiotape number K6312.01, http://tapes.millercenter.virginia.edu/pages/listen_tapes_lbj_tel.htm

p. 83, "Every person . . . on the floor . . . civil rights bill." Gittinger and Fisher, "LBJ Champions the Civil Rights Act," *Prologue*. National Archives website.

p. 84, "You want him . . . kind." Lyndon Baines Johnson and Everett Dirksen, audiotape number K6312.10 of telephone conversation, December 20, 1963, Miller Center, http://tapes.millercenter.virginia.edu/pages/listen_tapes_lbj_tel.htm

p. 84, "I don't want . . . he's a negro." Lyndon B. Johnson tapes, John Holliman, "Tapes reveal LBJ's support for civil rights," CNN Interactive, October 16, 1996. www.cnn.com/US/9610/16/lbj.tapes/index.html

p. 84, "I can't have . . . any integrated." Johnson tapes, Holliman, "Tapes reveal LBJ's support for civil rights," CNN Interactive.

p. 85, "I've never seen . . . church people." Anthony Lewis, "President Spurs Drive for House to Act on Rights," *New York Times*, December 4, 1963, 1.

pp. 85–86, "Liberal Republican John Lindsay . . . eight or ten days." E. W. Kenworthy, "Rights Bill Move Set for January," *New York Times*, December 6, 1963, 1.

p. 86, "little grounds for optimism . . . may even get results." "We Cannot Hesitate," *New York Times*, December 8, 1963, 242.

## Chapter Seven

p. 87, "Let this session . . . fair and final vote." E. W. Kenworthy, "President Pitches His Voice Low and Hopes High," *New York Times*, January 9, 1964, 1.

p. 88, "shortsighted and disastrous, . . . weapon at our disposal." John D. Morris, "Message Viewed as Election Key," *New York Times*, January 9, 1964, 1.

p. 89, "President Kennedy . . . Johnson does." Claude Sitton, "Civil Rights: New Crises Are Feared Because of Congressional Delays on Measure," *New York Times*, January 12, 1964, E3.

p. 89, "I have been here . . . pretty soon." E. W. Kenworthy, "House to Debate Rights Next Week," *New York Times*, January 24, 1964, 1.

p. 90, "I usually . . . 'Yes, dear.'" Flora Davis, *Moving the Mountain: The Women's Movement in America Since 1960*, New York: Simon and Schuster, 1991, 42.

p. 90, "If you do not . . . rights at all." Davis, *Moving the Mountain*, 43.

p. 91, "Two days later, . . . Act of 1964." Jo Freeman, "How 'Sex' Got into Title VII: Persistent Opportunism as a Maker of Public Policy," *Law and Inequality: A Journal of Theory and Practice* 9, no. 2, March 1991, 163–184.

p. 93, "If we can lock . . . business." Hubert H. Humphrey and Lyndon B. Johnson, audiotape number WH6402.19 of telephone conversation, January 23, 1964, Miller Center, http://tapes.millercenter.virginia.edu/pages/listen_tapes_lbj_tel.htm

p. 93, "Assistant Attorney General . . . for the bill." Ted Gittinger and Allen Fisher, "LBJ Champions the Civil Rights Act of 1964," *Prologue Magazine* 36, no. 2, Summer 2004. National Archives website: www.archives.gov/publications/prologue/2004/summer/civil-rights-act-1.html

p. 94, "He assigned . . . to be patient." Dan Cohen, *Undefeated: The Life of Hubert H. Humphrey*, Minneapolis: Lerner Publications, 1978, 240–241.

p. 95, "I think Senator . . . this legislation." Gittinger and Fisher, "LBJ Champions the Civil Rights Act," *Prologue*. National Archives website.

p. 96, "He changed his mind . . . of the amendment." Freeman, "How 'Sex' Got into Title VII," *Law and Inequality*, 163–184.

p. 96, "The National Council . . . of the act." Gittinger and Fisher, "LBJ Champions the Civil Rights Act," *Prologue*. National Archives website.

p. 97, "On May 14 . . . the changes." Cohen, *Undefeated*, 241.

p. 98, "I have had . . . cloture." "Everett McKinley Dirksen's Finest Hour: June 10, 1964." *Peoria Journal Star*, June 10, 2004. Dirksen Congressional Center website, www.dirksencenter.org/print_basics_histmats_civilrights64_cloturespeech.htm

p. 98, "Shortly after . . . history." E. W. Kenworthy, "Senate Invokes Cloture on Rights Bill, 71 to 29, Ending 75-Day Filibuster," *New York Times*, June 11, 1964, 1.

p. 99, "Two days after . . . 'an old Halleck man.'" Lyndon Baines Johnson and Charles Halleck, audiotape of telephone conversation, June 21, 1964, Miller Center, http://millercenter.org/academic/presidentialrecordings/pages/clips.htm

p. 100, "Proclaim liberty . . . thereof." E. W. Kenworthy, "President Signs Civil Rights Bill; Bids All to Back It," *New York Times*, July 3, 1964, 1, 9.

p. 100, "During the debate . . . *New York Times* report." Kenworthy, "President Signs Civil Rights Bill," *Times*, 1, 9.

pp. 100, 103, "heedless trampling . . . bitterness." Kenworthy, "President Signs Civil Rights Bill," *Times*, 1, 9.

pp. 101–102, Civil Rights Act, July 2, 1964, U.S. Statutes at Large, Public Law 88-352, 241–268, The Avalon Project at Yale Law School, www.yale.edu/lawweb/avalon/statutes/civil_rights_1964.htm

p. 103, "At around 2 p.m., . . . 136 were Republicans," Kenworthy, "President Signs Civil Rights Bill," *Times*, 1, 9.

p. 103, "It was a great . . . Abraham Lincoln." Martin Luther King Jr., quoted in Nicolaus Mills, "Who Passed the Civil Rights Act of 1964?" *Dissent* magazine, Winter 2008, www.alternet.org/rights/77507

pp. 104–105, "Those who . . . our nation whole." *Public Papers of the Presidents of the United States: Lyndon B. Johnson*, 1963–64. II: 446, Washington, DC:

GPO, 1965, 842–844. www.lbjlib.utexas.edu/johnson/archives.hom/speeches. hom/640702.asp

p. 105, "the most sweeping . . . this country." Kenworthy, "President Signs Civil Rights Bill," *Times*, 1, 9.

## Chapter Eight

p. 108, "more impact . . . twentieth century." Quoted in Ted Gittinger and Allen Fisher, "LBJ Champions the Civil Rights Act of 1964," *Prologue Magazine* 36, no. 2, Summer 2004. National Archives website: www.archives.gov/publications/ prologue/2004/summer/civil-rights-act-1.html

pp. 109–110, "the liberty . . . and liberty." Oral arguments, *Heart of Atlanta* v. *United States*, 379 U.S. 241 (1964).

p. 110, "'There was ample' . . . subjected to slavery." Oral arguments, *Heart of Atlanta*, 379 U.S. 241.

pp. 110–111, "The Court, . . . 'governmental regulation.'" *Heart of Atlanta*, 379 U.S. 241.

p. 111, "Instead of the resistance . . . with the law." Anthony Lewis, "Civil Rights: Decade of Progress," *New York Times*, December 20, 1964, E3.

p. 112, "Much can . . . to obtain." *King Encyclopedia*, Stanford University, www. stanford.edu/group/King/about_king/encyclopedia/voting_rights_act.htm

p. 113, "Freedom is not enough, . . . civil rights." Lyndon B. Johnson, "To Fulfill These Rights," Commencement Address, Howard University, June 4, 1965, www. lbjlib.utexas.edu/johnson/archives.hom/speeches.hom/650604.asp

p. 113, "been a critical . . . single generation." Joseph Califano, "What Was Really Great About the Great Society," *Washington Monthly*, October 1999.

pp. 113–114, "When the Civil Rights . . . student body." "Integration: The 1964 Civil Rights Act to the Present." "Integration," *The Columbia Electronic Encyclopedia*, 2000–2007, Pearson Education, publishing as Infoplease.

p. 114, "Today's education . . . for many students." Neil Schoenherr, "'Today's education system is still segregated and in need of major improvements,' says urban school reform expert," News & Information, Washington University in St. Louis, April 9, 2004. http://news-info.wustl.edu/tips/page/normal/834.html

p. 114, "The Civil Rights Act . . . to desegregate." Center for American Progress, "The Civil Rights Act 40 Years Later," Center for American Progress, July 2, 2004, www.americanprogress.org/issues/2004/07/b106855.html

p. 115, "The Act was groundbreaking . . . Americans." "The Civil Rights Act." www. americanprogress.org/issues/2004/07/b106855.html

p. 115, "The fights . . . day to this." Michael Oreskes, "Civil Rights Act Leaves Deep Mark on the American Political Landscape," *New York Times*, July 3, 1989, 1.

p. 115, "I think we . . . time to come." Clarence Page, "Essay: Politics of Division," *Online NewsHour*, PBS, August 30, 2005, www.pbs.org/newshour/essays/july–dec05/page_8-30.html

p. 116, "Two million more . . . in 2004." Sam Roberts, "2008 Surge in Black Voters Nearly Erased Racial Gap," *New York Times*, July 20, 2009.

p. 116, "95 percent . . . Obama." Megan Thee, "Multiple Signs of a Changing Electorate," *New York Times*, November 6, 2008.

pp. 116, 119, "In the 1950s . . . national average." Lisa Cozzens, "The Civil Rights Movement 1955–1965." *African American History*. http://fledge.watson.org/~lisa/blackhistory/civilrights-55-65 (25 May 1998).

p. 117, "a national catharsis . . . American politics." Adam Nagourney, "Obama Elected President as Racial Barrier Falls," *New York Times*, November 5, 2008, 1.

pp. 117–118, "The Door Has Been Opened," Author interview/eye-witness account, January 20, 2009, Washington, D.C.

p. 120, "is also one . . . to do so." Center for American Progress, "The Civil Rights Act." www.americanprogress.org/issues/2004/07/b106855.html

p. 120, "Civil rights abuses . . . violent crimes." Jennifer L. Eberhardt, Paul G. Davies, Valerie J. Purdie–Vaughns, and Sheri Lynn Johnson, "Looking Deathworthy: Perceived Stereotypicality of Black Defendants Predicts Capital–Sentencing Outcomes," *Psychological Science*, 17:5 (2006).

p. 121, "Women continue . . . male workers," Alice H. Eagly and Linda L. Carli, *Through the Labyrinth: The Truth About How Women Become Leaders*, Cambridge, MA: Harvard Business School Press, 2007, 68,

p. 121, "Only 2 percent . . . those companies." Eagly and Carli, 19.

p. 121, "Civil rights . . . of America." Center for American Progress, "The Civil Rights Act." www.americanprogress.org/issues/2004/07/b106855.html

pp. 122–125, "From Bill to Law." Bernard Asbell, *The Senate Nobody Knows*, Baltimore: Johns Hopkins University Press, 1978; Charles W. Johnson, "How Our Laws Are Made," Washington, D.C.: U.S. Government Printing Office, 1998; and "Measures of Congressional Workload," CongressLink, The Dirksen Congressional Center, www.congresslink.org/print_basics_histmats_workloadstats.htm

All websites accessible as of April 1, 2009.

# Further Information

## BOOKS

Colbert, Nancy A. *Great Society: The Story of Lyndon Baines Johnson.* Greensboro, NC: Morgan Reynolds Inc., 2002.

George, Charles, ed. *Living Through the Civil Rights Movement.* San Diego, CA: Greenhaven Press, 2006.

Gold, Susan Dudley. Brown *v.* Board of Education*: Separate but Equal?* New York: Marshall Cavendish, 2006.

Hardy, Sheila Jackson, and P. Stephen Hardy. *Extraordinary People of the Civil Rights Movement.* Danbury, CT: Children's Press, 2007.

Hasday, Judy L. *The Civil Rights Act of 1964: An End to Racial Segregation.* New York: Chelsea House Publications, 2007.

Karson, Jill. *Civil Rights.* San Diego, CA: Greenhaven Press, 2003.

King, Martin Luther Jr. *The Autobiography of Martin Luther King, Jr.* New York: Grand Central Publishing, 2001.

Levy, Debbie. *Lyndon B. Johnson.* Minneapolis, MN: Lerner Publishing Group, 2002.

Mayer, Robert H. *The Civil Rights Act of 1964.* San Diego, CA: Greenhaven Press, 2004.

McNeese, Tim. *The Civil Rights Movement: Striving for Justice.* New York: Chelsea House Publications, 2007.

Miller, Calvin Craig. *No Easy Answers: Bayard Rustin and the Civil Rights Movement.* Greensboro, NC: Morgan Reynolds Publishing, 2005.

Skog, Jason. *The Civil Rights Act of 1964.* Williamsport, PA: Compass Point Books, 2007.

# The Civil Rights Act of 1964

Wright, Susan. *The Civil Rights Act of 1964*. New York: Rosen Central, 2005.

Young, Mitchell, ed. *Racial Discrimination*. San Diego, CA: Greenhaven Press, 2006.

## WEBSITES

**The African–American Mosaic**
www.loc.gov/exhibits/african/intro.html
A collection of Library of Congress resources on black history and culture

**African American Odyssey: The Civil Rights Era**
http://memory.loc.gov/ammem/aaohtml/exhibit/aopart9.html

**AfricanAmericans.com**
www.africanamericans.com
Culture and history of African Americans and a section on civil rights.

**The American President: Lyndon Baines Johnson**
www.millercenter.virginia.edu/index.php/academic/americanpresident/
lbjohnson
Speeches, essays, private and public papers, multimedia presentations, and Lyndon Johnson's private White House tapes.

**The Dirksen Congressional Center**
www.congresslink.org/

**The Lyndon Baines Johnson Library and Museum**
www.lbjlib.utexas.edu
Speeches, tapes, multimedia presentations, and oral histories by many of Lyndon Johnson's friends and associates.

**National Association for the Advancement of Colored People (NAACP)**
www.naacp.org

**U.S. House of Representatives**
www.house.gov

**U.S. Senate**
www.senate.gov

**U.S. Supreme Court cases and audiotapes of oral arguments**
www.oyez.org

# Bibliography

## ARTICLES

Calabresi, Steven. Testimony before the U.S. Senate's Committee on the Judiciary, May 6, 2003. www.freerepublic.com/focus/f-news/907801/posts

"The Civil Rights Act of 1960." AfricanAmericans.com. www.africanamericans.com/CivilRightsActof1960.htm

"Filibuster and Cloture." U.S. Senate website. www.senate.gov/artandhistory/history/common/briefing/Filibuster_Cloture.htm

Freeman, Jo. "How 'Sex' Got into Title VII: Persistent Opportunism as a Maker of Public Policy." *Law and Inequality: A Journal of Theory and Practice* 9, no. 2 (March 1991), 163–184.

Gittinger, Ted, and Allen Fisher. "LBJ Champions the Civil Rights Act of 1964." *Prologue Magazine* 36, no. 2 (Summer 2004). www.archives.gov/publications/prologue/2004/summer/civil-rights-act-1.html

Holliman, John. "Tapes reveal LBJ's support for civil rights," CNN Interactive (October 16, 1996). www.cnn.com/US/9610/16/lbj.tapes/index.html

Johnson, Charles W. "How Our Laws Are Made" (Washington, DC: GPO, 1998). *New York Times* articles, 1963–1964; 2007.

## BOOKS

Califano, Joseph A. Jr. *The Triumph & Tragedy of Lyndon Johnson.* New York: Simon & Schuster, 1991.

Caro, Robert A. *Master of the Senate: The Years of Lyndon Johnson.* New York: Random House, 2002

Cohen, Dan. *Undefeated: The Life of Hubert H. Humphrey.* Minneapolis: Lerner Publications Company, 1978.

Dallek, Robert. *Flawed Giant, Lyndon Johnson and His Times 1961–1975.* New York: Oxford University Press, 1998.

Davis, Flora. *Moving the Mountain: The Women's Movement in America Since 1960*. New York: Simon and Schuster, 1991.

Evans, Rowland, and Robert Novak. *Lyndon B. Johnson: The Exercise of Power*. New York: New American Library, 1966.

Goodwin, Doris Kearns. *Lyndon Johnson and the American Dream*. New York: St. Martin's Press, 1991.

Johnson, Lyndon Baines. *The Vantage Point, Perspectives of the Presidency 1963–1969*. New York: Holt, Rinehart and Winston, 1971.

## COURT CASES
*Brown v. Board of Education of Topeka, Kansas*, 347 U.S. 483 (1954).

*Civil Rights Cases*, 109 U.S. 3 (1883).

*Ex parte Milligan*, 71 U.S. 2 (1866).

## DOCUMENTS AND FEDERAL STATUTES
U. S. Const. amendment XIII

U. S. Const. amendment XIV

U. S. Const. amendment XV

*Civil Rights Act of 1957*, Pub. L. No. 85-315. 71 Stat. 634.

*Civil Rights Act of 1960*, Pub. L. No. 86-449. 74 Stat. 86.

U.S. Congress. House, *Civil Rights Act of 1963*, H. Doc. 124, 88th Cong., 1st sess.

*Civil Rights Act of 1964*, Pub. L. No. 88-352. 78 Stat. 241.

*Civil Rights Act of 1968*, Pub. L. No. 109-136. 119 Stat. 2643.

*Equal Rights Amendment (ERA)*, several versions proposed but not ratified

Southern Manifesto

U.S. Const. art. 1, § 8, cl. 3 (Commerce Clause)

## INTERVIEWS/RECORDINGS
Cooper, Stephen. Lyndon Johnson's Press Conferences, 1980. Education Resources Information Center. www.eric.ed.gov. Accessed Sept. 2, 2007.

Interview with Glennon Threatt, June 16, 2005. Interview U-0023. Southern Oral History Program Collection (#4007), http://docsouth.unc.edu/sohp/U-0023/U-0023.html

"The Legacy of Medgar Evers." *All Things Considered*, NPR (June 10, 2003).

Lyndon B. Johnson tapes. Miller Center. http://tapes.millercenter.virginia.edu/pages/listen_tapes_lbj_tel.htm

Lyndon B. Johnson tapes. Ponce, Phil, "Caught on Tape." *The Online NewsHour*, PBS (October 14, 1997). www.pbs.org/newshour/bb/white_house/july-dec97/lbj_10-14.html

Oral History Interview, Internet Copy, LBJ Library. www.lbjlib.utexas.edu

## WEBSITES
Dirksen Congressional Center
www.congresslink.org

Library of Congress, American Memory section.
http://memory.loc.gov/ammem/collections

Lyndon Baines Johnson Library.
www.lbjlib.utexas.edu

Miller Center's site on Lyndon B. Johnson.
www.millercenter.virginia.edu/index.php/academic/americanpresident/lbjohnson

National Archives and Records Administration.
www.archives.gov

U.S. House of Representatives
www.house.gov/

U.S. Senate
www.senate.gov/

All websites accessible as of April 1, 2009.

# Index

Page numbers in **boldface** are photographs.

# About the Author

SUSAN DUDLEY GOLD has worked as a reporter for a daily newspaper, managing editor of two statewide business magazines, and freelance writer for several regional publications. She has written more than four dozen books for middle-school and high-school students on a variety of topics, including American history, health issues, law, and space.

Gold has won numerous awards for her work, including most recently the selection of Loving *v.* Virginia: *Lifting the Ban Against Interracial Marriage*, part of Marshall Cavendish's Supreme Court Milestones series, as one of the Notable Social Studies Trade Books for Young People in 2009. Two other books in that series were recognized in 2008: United States *v.* Amistad: *Slave Ship Mutiny*, selected as a Carter G. Woodson Honor Book, and Tinker *v.* Des Moines: *Free Speech for Students*, awarded first place in the National Federation of Press Women's communications contest, nonfiction juvenile book category.

Gold has written several titles in the Landmark Legislation series for Marshall Cavendish. She is the author of several books on Maine history. She and her husband, John Gold, own and operate a web design and publishing business in Maine. They have one son, Samuel.